radically
unchurched

radically
unchurched

WHO THEY ARE & HOW TO REACH THEM

alvin l. reid

Kregel
Academic & Professional

Radically Unchurched: Who They Are & How To Reach Them

© 2002 by Alvin L. Reid

Published by Kregel Publications, P.O. Box 2607, Grand Rapids, MI 49501.

Scripture quotations marked KJV are from the King James Version of the Holy Bible.

Scripture quotations marked NIV are from the Holy Bible, New International Version®. © 1973, 1978, 1984 by International Bible Society. Used by permission of Zondervan Publishing House. All rights reserved.

Scripture quotations marked NKJV are from the *New King James Version.* © 1979, 1980, 1982, Thomas Nelson, Inc., Publishers.

Scripture quotations marked NASB are from the New American Standard Bible, © the Lockman Foundation 1960, 1962, 1963, 1968, 1971, 1972, 1973, 1975, 1977.

Library of Congress Cataloging-in-Publication Data
Reid, Alvin L.
    Radically unchurched: who they are and how to reach them / by Alvin L. Reid
        p. cm.
Includes bibliographical references and indexes.
    1. Non church-affiliated people—United States.
2. Evangelistic work—United States. I. Title.
BR526 .R445   2002
266'.00973—dc21   2002006246

ISBN 978-0-8254-3633-8

To my students at Southeastern Baptist Theological Seminary for their incomparable encouragement. And to all the graduates of Southeastern as well as all others who minister in the name of Christ, with a burden to penetrate the unchurched culture in America. May God multiply workers in His harvest fields.

Contents

Foreword

IS IT POSSIBLE TO COMPOSE A thoughtful, provocative, and genuinely helpful book on evangelizing in the contemporary milieu? Could such a work accurately depict the philosophical landscape, both popular and academic, and address that vista with theological precision and captivating readability? By most anyone's judgment, this does not happen very often; but Alvin Reid has splendidly succeeded here.

The Radically Unchurched: Who They Are and How to Reach Them is a book about sharing Christ in the rapidly changing scene that threatens to engulf and capsize the church today. The vast majority of the history of North America is the history of the church of Jesus Christ addressing the gospel to folks who had at least a vestigial memory of Christian perspectives. Native Americans and slaves were exceptions, but most other immigrants arriving in the new world were from nations boasting a Christian heritage. Evangelists and witnesses had a foundation on which to build. Sometimes there was some "Jeremiah work" to do, plucking up, pulling down, . . . and destroying (Jer. 1:10). But if Jesus were mentioned, most people were not automatically ostracized from the conversation. And this era continued until the cessation of hostilities at the end of World War II.

But when Johnny came marching home from Europe in 1945, he was different. More than two Japanese cities went up in the mushroom clouds at Hiroshima and Nagasaki. Innocence and hope had eroded into doubt and cynicism. Soldiers trooping home from Korea and Vietnam were still more disillusioned. These merely reflected the perspectives of the general public.

Add to this the serial immorality of multiplied hero athletes, political leaders, and, pray God forgive us, high- and low-profile clergymen, all purporting to be followers of Jesus of Nazareth, and public doubt is hardly surprising. Sprinkle in a heavy dose of 1960s insanity; the failed promises of psychotherapy; the dawning of postmodern relativism; large infusions of new immigrants from Hindu, Buddhist, and Islamic cultures; and the quasi-demise of most well-known Christian denominations. The product is a culture of what Alvin Reid calls the "radically unchurched."

Professor Reid is at home with such a generation. In effect, he leads two lives. He is a fine husband, good father, circumspect professor, and observant churchman—by day. By night, he is . . . well, unusual. He handles snakes (not religiously but for fun), mixes with any sort of company, understands and even appreciates the contemporary music scene, and talks to the antiquated like me and to high school and college students with the same alacrity.

This foot-in-both-worlds posture is what makes this book critically important. Professor Reid knows what it takes to reach the radically unchurched. He does it all the time. He knows how and where the church must change if it is ever to fulfill our Lord's command in the "land of the free and the home of the brave." He comprehends the distinction between that part of Christianity that cannot be altered without changing its basic character, and the accretions of tradition that can and often should be jettisoned. He knows that the leopard cannot change his spots, and he has no desire to make it do so. But he also knows that you can breed a sleeker, faster, stronger, more efficient leopard and that is precisely what this book is about.

If your "cup of tea" is the humdrum of church as usual, or if you are content simply to live your life among the existing saints, then do not dare read this volume. Do not even pick it up. It is more dangerous to your future than those serpents Professor Reid carries around his neck. But, if you are set on adventure, believe that one ought to take Jesus at His Word, share His gospel with all people, and have a hankering to see your church set ablaze with love, excitement, and renewed holiness, plop your money down, donate your change to the first "radically unchurched" to whom you witness, and read one book that will change your life and church.

—PAIGE PATTERSON, President
Southeastern Baptist Theological Seminary
Wake Forest, North Carolina

Preface

IN 1999, LEADERS OF THE Southern Baptist Convention planned a major evangelistic effort for the summer of 2000 in the city of Chicago. Since evangelism lies at the heart of Southern Baptists, such an effort is hardly remarkable. What made this particular endeavor noteworthy was the response of the Council of Religious Leaders of Metropolitan Chicago. They wrote a letter of protest to Paige Patterson, president of Southeastern Baptist Theological Seminary, who at the time was president of the Southern Baptist Convention. In their letter of November 27, the council said that the evangelistic plans could lead to "hate crimes," and they urged Southern Baptists not to send volunteers to "seek converts in Chicago."[1]

The council's response sounds more like the Sadducees speaking to the apostles in Acts 4 than it does one supposedly Christian group speaking to another in modern America. Many in the Church, however, have lost their passion and conviction about the gospel, resulting in such controversy.

When the nature of the Christian mission causes a stir among those who claim to be Christians, it's time to reevaluate what it means to be Christian. Recently, one of my students, Andre, met a Muslim student at a local university. Andre began witnessing to the student, who had only recently come to the States. The student asked Andre if, since he claimed to be a Christian, he slept with his girlfriend. "No!" my student replied incredulously. "Why would you ask that?" The Muslim student replied, "Because America is a Christian nation, and every student I know [here] sleeps with his girlfriend." While an extreme example, this conversation demonstrates the confusion—among both believers and nonbelievers—in regard to Christianity.

This book does not directly address the problem of America's losing her Christian identity. Rather, it examines one of the underlying causes of this loss—and its result, namely, the failure of the American church to follow the New Testament pattern of penetrating the culture with the gospel. This examination is, however, positive; rather than merely complain about the problem I offer a remedy for it.

My background consists of two closely related worlds. First, evangelism is my passion. This book encourages evangelicals to look to the fields, especially those fields ripe with the souls of the radically unchurched. Second, I teach and write on the subject of spiritual awakenings, and on a few occasions I've seen a glimpse of what happens when God moves in power in a church or on a campus. And the best way to penetrate the culture is through a mighty movement of God.

Because of my years of leadership experience within the Southern Baptist Convention, you will find that several examples used in this text refer to affiliated churches. The Southern Baptist Convention has also done much valuable research on evangelism and church growth, which is refered to at times in this manuscript. Please be assured, however, that the material presented is relevant regardless of your denomination.

It is my hope that this book will give the reader a passion to pray for a mighty awakening in our lifetime—an awakening on both a personal and corporate level. On a personal level, many Christians in America have met Jesus Christ in a genuine life-changing way—but they've gotten over it! The greatest need in the church is for a radical, fanatical, passionate band of believers to assault the darkness in our society with the light of the gospel. Our generation has so compartmentalized faith that what we profess only rarely matches how we live. The net result has been an abject failure to penetrate the unchurched culture. On a corporate level, we in

America simply cannot continue to "do church" as we've done for the past thirty or forty years. True, over the past forty years many churches in this country have brought great glory to God. But the impact of the church has waned, particularly in her ability to reach into the subcultures of the unchurched.

My prayer is that these pages will encourage you to abandon yourself to live for God, but not you alone. I pray that the light of your spirit and that of others like you, fed by the Spirit of God moving in you, will flame together and penetrate the darkness of the unchurched in America. If we don't do it, no one will. This book may not contain all the answers about how to reach the unchurched, but it raises many of the right questions.

For those interested in teaching the concepts of this book to a group or congregation, a companion workbook which goes hand-in-hand with the text can be purchased through oraclepublishing.org.

Acknowledgments

THE WORDS OF THIS BOOK, although mine, flow from several streams of influence, dating back to my early days in the ministry. So many people—far more than I can name—have influenced my passion to reach the unchurched. Some are especially dear: my pastor in college, Wayne Watts; my evangelism professors in seminary, Roy Fish, Jim Eaves, Malcolm McDow, and Dan Crawford; Jerry Sutton, my pastor at a critical time in seminary; and my president at Southeastern Baptist Theological Seminary, Paige Patterson, who exemplifies the need of our day—people who are committed to sound belief and practice. His encouragement to me is unparalleled.

Fenton Moorhead, my pastor in Houston, and my current pastor Richard Mills have demonstrated how a pastor can lead his church to reach the unchurched. A special thanks to those who've helped me think through what I want to say in this book. My colleague Bill Brown has been particularly helpful with chapter 12 as well as with insights throughout the book. Matt Queen and Larry MacDonald, doctoral students of mine, have given thoughtful advice. Lori Calloway read the manuscript and gave excellent pointers on practical matters.

My secretaries, Julie Meeks, Laura Fuller, and Denise Quinn, have been tireless in their typing and retyping of the manuscript. Other individuals read the manuscript and offered excellent suggestions, although any shortcomings are my own.

I thank my president, my hero, and mentor, Paige Patterson. I could never imagine having a better boss in this life. To my precious family—Michelle, the love of my life, and the greatest kids on earth, Josh and Hannah—thanks once again for putting up with my endless hours on the laptop computer. This book is as much yours as it is mine.

part one

A Profile of the Radically Unchurched

A BOY AND GIRL WENT ON their first date. Afterwards, at her front door, the boy said, "Can I kiss you?"

The girl smiled and said nothing.

The boy tried again, "I mean, *may* I kiss you?"

Again she smiled and said nothing.

"Are you dead?" the exasperated boy uttered.

"Are you paralyzed?" she replied.[1]

Looking at the impact of the church on American culture in the past generation, one gets the impression that she's been paralyzed, as if waiting for permission to act. The moral downslide in this country has become an avalanche. For many, spirituality can be characterized as a cafeteria of "make-your-own-religion." The Judeo-Christian heritage that helped to establish America has become increasingly marginalized.

Part 1 of this book is a wakeup call to the church to return to her first love—a passion for Jesus. Leonard Sweet recounts Steve Allen's story, which illustrates the need for authentic Christianity. Allen describes two upper-middle-class suburbanites named Danny and Hank:

Danny: I feel guilty about being dissatisfied with my life. After all, what right do I have to expect things to be better than they are?

Hank: You're asking some pretty pervasive questions. . . . The fact is, we are all hung up with things, and then people retreat further from what is really important by leaning on religion.

Danny: Don't you think religion has a reality of its own?

Hank: Sure, but there isn't one churchgoer in a thousand who ever perceives what the founder of his or her religion has in mind. Your average churchgoer is not looking for enlightenment; your average churchgoer is looking for security.[2]

Ouch. What a sad but apt depiction of the church today. We seek security, not enlightenment. But God is raising up a fresh generation of believers, both young and old, who seek not only God's hand—they seek God's face. These believers want to be a part of the solution rather than a part of the problem. A rising tide of God's children desires to saturate the unchurched world with the hope of the gospel. Read on and join in their number.

chapter one

A Brave New
World(liness)

Who Are the Radically Unchurched?

Radically changed DESCRIBES the effect of the gospel on young Bill. His combination of wild hair, torn jeans, shoeless feet, and tie-dyed T-shirt testifies to how recent was his conversion to Christianity.

His appearance, though, belies his unusual intelligence, and on a particular Sunday soon after his conversion, Bill attended a local congregation for fellowship and nurture beyond his college Bible study. Across the street from the campus sat the college church, filled weekly with well-dressed and conservative members. The church earnestly desired to develop a ministry to the students, but hadn't yet done so. They were uncertain how to go about it.

Picture the scene as Bill enters. He has no shoes. He is clad in his jeans, T-shirt, and sports that wild hair. The service has already started, so Bill ambles down the aisle looking for a seat. The pews are full, so he keeps walking. By now, people are a bit uncomfortable, but no one says anything. Bill continues down the aisle, looking for a seat, but finds only perplexed gazes. When he realizes there are no seats, he simply squats down on the floor. At the college fellowship, this is perfectly acceptable, but no one had ever done it at this church.

The people grow nervous and the tension thickens. Then a deacon rises from his seat and slowly makes his way toward Bill. This particular deacon is in his eighties, has silver-gray hair, wears a three-piece suit, accented by a pocket watch. Known as a godly man, elegant, dignified, and courtly, his gait is aided by a finely crafted cane. As the deacon walks toward Bill, many are thinking, *You can't blame him for what he's going to do. How can a man of his age and background understand some college kid?*

It takes a long time for the deacon to reach Bill. Silence reigns; one can almost hear the tapping of the deacon's cane. All eyes focus upon him, and the people are thinking, *The minister can't even preach the sermon until the deacon does what he has to do.*

Suddenly, the elderly man drops his cane to the floor. With great difficulty he lowers himself and sits next to Bill. When the pastor has regained his voice he says, "What I'm about to preach, you may never remember. What you have just seen, you will never forget."[1]

Is *your* church more aptly described as a hotel for saints, or a hospital for sinners?

In 90 percent of evangelical churches, most deacons or congregations would *not* have responded to young Bill as did the deacon in the above scenario. We've lost a sense of compassion in America for the radically unchurched, and that's why so few lost people, or even new believers like Bill, are found in most of our churches. Most Christians in America see the church as a hotel for saints rather than a hospital for sinners. The church has, by and large, failed to be salt and light in the midst of a depraved humanity. That failure contributed to the tragedy at Columbine. An apparent intention of the so-called Trenchcoat Mafia was to murder professing believers at Columbine, an intent that demonstrates the lostness of the unchurched youth who fill our public schools. What more will it take before the church awakens to the depth of that lostness? Must armed and hostile unbelievers invade our Sunday services before we awaken to the Great Commission?

The dawning of the church's third millennium A.D. demands serious reflection. What stands as the single most pressing need for the church as it relates to evangelism? The escalation of violence in schools, as horrific as it is, illustrates an even worse reality—the lostness of people, the numbers of lost people, that the name of Jesus has *not* penetrated the unchurched culture.

Who Are the Radically Unchurched?

The *radically unchurched* are those who have no clear personal understanding of the message of the gospel, and who have had little or no contact with a Bible-teaching, Christ-honoring church. The number of radically unchurched grows each year, while the church's ability to penetrate the culture seems to be waning. Chip Arn reports the following statistics:[2] active, practicing Christians compose—even when being generous with the numbers—only 82.08 million or 29 percent of the population in the United States.[3] Those Christian in name only (giving no evidence of any consistent practice of their faith) comprise 86.07 million or 30 percent. Americans who report no religious affiliation total 116.85 million or 41 percent. The largest percentage consists of the last group the radically unchurched. George Hunter is the author of *Church for the Unchurched.* Hunter's term *secular people*—that is, persons "who have navigated their whole lives beyond the serious influence of Christian churches"[4]—is similar to my definition of *radically unchurched.* Hunter states that approximately 120 million Americans fit the category.

Radically unchurched—people who have no clear personal understanding of the message of the gospel, and who have had little or no contact with a Bible-teaching, Christ-honoring church.

Radically Unchurched Described

An analogy can best describe the radically unchurched.[5] In the first century, the apostle Paul was called of God as a missionary to the Gentiles. The Jews were Paul's people. They had a heritage of faith, a scriptural underpinning, and a common cultural background. The Gentiles in the first century were those who, for the most part, knew nothing about the gospel message until someone like Paul told them. Some Gentiles were religious; some were not. But they had no heritage of Scripture, as did the Jews.

First-century Gentiles, then, are analogous to the millions of unchurched people in our day in this country who have almost no real knowledge of Christianity. Oh, they know what a clerical collar is, and they recognize a church building, but they have no practical knowledge of the gospel. They may even be devoutly religious; they may be Muslim or Hindu or New Age or Mormon. Or they may be agnostic. The difference between the unchurched and nominal Christians—comparable to Jews in the analogy—is that their perceptions of Christianity are obscure or terribly flawed.

Two Groups of Unbelievers in the United States

Group I	Group II
Nominals =	Radically Unchurched=
to first-century Jews	to first-century Gentiles

To some of the radically unchurched McDonald's golden arches present a symbol that has more meaning than does a cross. So if Arn's statistics are correct—and if anything they are inflated toward Christian practice—the following could be said: New Testament, genuine believers comprise 29 percent of the U.S. population; the nominally churched, 30 percent; the radically unchurched, 41 percent. Little evidence reflects that significant inroads are being made by the church to reach the largest statistical category.

The Southern Baptist Convention evangelizes with arguably as much or more passion and effectiveness than does any other Christian denomination. Yet each year between six thousand to eight thousand Southern Baptist churches report baptizing no new converts. And of the thirty thousand-plus churches in the Convention that do reach people for Christ, very few effectively penetrate the radically unchurched. According to a 1993 study by the North American Mission Board, only one in nine adults who were baptized described themselves as unchurched. In other words, eight of nine—almost 90 percent—of baptized adults had a connection with a church.[6]

The decline in reaching new converts is far more serious when one examines the effectiveness of all churches in America to reach the radically unchurched. Hunter notes that of the over 350,000 churches in the U.S., about 80 percent are stagnant. Of the 20 percent that are growing, most increase by biological (babies born to current members) or transfer growth. Less than 1 percent is growing by conversion growth. So a minuscule fraction of the radically unchurched is being reached. This reality alone merits calling for a national day of fasting, prayer, and public humiliation before the Lord, who deserves far better.

Hunter asserts that the growth in the number of radically unchurched results from a half-millennium-long process of secularization: "Secularization, defined as the withdrawal of whole areas of life and thought from the church's influence, was present for 500 years and continues unchecked."[7] By the end of the twentieth century, says Hunter, Christianity especially enjoyed less and less of a "home field advantage" when in regard to sharing its message of the gospel. Thus, a whole generation of people have "little or no Christian memory background or vocabulary. Many of them do not even know what we are talking about, and have little or no experience of church."[8]

The Effect of the Waning Influence of the Church

In increasing numbers, Americans are pouring through the spiritual down spout and into the cesspool of biblical ignorance. In 1952, only 6 percent of adults had received no religious training during childhood. Church growth writer Chip Arn notes that by 1965 that figure had increased slightly to 9 percent. By 1978 it jumped to 17 percent. Only three years later, in 1981, 21 percent of adults reported their having no religious instruction during childhood. By 1993 the number had ballooned to 35 percent.[9] Arn examines the implications of these numbers. First, people are increasingly unfamiliar with religious words, symbols, or rituals. Yet the church is using the terminology of fifty years ago. Second, America is a media-dominated society, yet the church lags behind the culture in the use of technology. Third, American values are dominated by secularism. We cannot assume all people believe like us. Finally, American society is increasingly fragmented. A new form of tribalism divides the nation like never before into subgroups.

Over the past decade, membership in Protestant churches dropped 9.5 percent, while the U.S. population grew 11 percent. Further, fewer than 1 percent of American churches grow by conversion. Why such a failure to reach the unchurched? The church will not reach the unchurched without changing. We cannot do church the way we have in the past.

Arn offers these observations about most American churches:

1. Reaching non-Christians is a low priority for most churches;
2. Reaching non-Christians is a low priority for most individual believers;
3. The biblical concept of *lostness* has disappeared from most churches and from the minds of most Christians;
4. Most evangelistic methods used today are ineffective in making disciples;
5. The church focuses on decisions over disciples;
6. Making disciples is interpreted to mean only spiritual growth.

Models of the Radically Unchurched Population

Before any discussion about reaching the radically unchurched, any faulty notions or stereotypes about this segment of the population should be addressed. In a groundbreaking study of the unchurched, Thom Rainer, Dean of the Billy Graham School of Missions, Evangelism, and

Church Growth, surveyed some seven hundred formerly unchurched believers to determine what factors helped them come to Christ. Included in his findings were nine myths about the unchurched:[10]

Myth 1: Most unchurched think and act like Anglo, middle-class suburbanites with no church background.

Myth 2: The unchurched are turned off by denominational names in the church name.

Myth 3: The unchurched never attend church.

Myth 4: The unchurched cannot be reached by direct personal evangelism.

Myth 5: If a church is to reach the unchurched, the pastor must be a dynamic and charismatic leader.

Myth 6: In our teaching and preaching we must not communicate complex biblical truths that will confuse the unchurched.

Myth 7: Sunday school and other small groups are ineffective in attracting the unchurched.

Myth 8: The most important evangelistic relationships take place in the marketplace.

Myth 9: The unchurched are concerned only about their own needs.

The radically unchurched population should not be seen as a monolithic group in America. Their diversity parallels that found in other demographic categories. Characteristics of the radically unchurched include the following:

- Some are religious, some are not.
- Some have strong moral convictions of some form, others do not.
- Some are well educated, some are illiterate.
- Some are wealthy, some live in poverty.

The radically unchurched may be urban or rural, speak one of over a hundred languages, and represent hundreds of ethnic origins. Some are passive, while others are militant. The radically unchurched cut across virtually every imaginable barrier except one—they have virtually no real, personal knowledge of the gospel. While there is no "typical" radically unchurched person, following are examples of the diversity represented by the radically unchurched.

The Devoutly Religious Unchurched

By radically unchurched, I do not mean irreligious. The vast majority of unchurched people worship some deity. If evangelism meant simply getting people to be religious, there would be little evangelizing to do! Many of the radically unchurched are second and third generation Muslim, Buddhist, and Hindu, but are often very Americanized. Adherents to all major religions can be found in any large American city. And not only in the cities. The owner of a fast food restaurant I visited in rural Georgia had brought a deep Hindu faith from his native India.

Multitudes are devoted also to New Age philosophies of one brand or another. Recently my wife shared Christ with a lady who was considering the purchase of a house in the area. The lady spent the night in her potential home, attempting to "see what the house said" to her. In my opinion, it said it needed a paint job. But she, like so many others, considered listening to a house to be a serious spiritual experience.

Still others seek God in one of hundreds of cults. The radically unchurched are not irreligious, but they are lost, separated from God. And these precious souls are everywhere:

- Bindu, a university student born in Asia and raised in Houston, devoutly Buddhist (but recently came to Christ!)
- Teresa, a twenty-one-year-old in New Hampshire who follows Wicca, mainly because there is no evangelical witness where she lives, and it is the religion of choice in her town
- Lucy, a New Age devotee who admires Jesus Christ as well as her crystals

---

Did You Know?
Did you know that Muslims now equal Jews in population in the U.S.? About 5 to 6 million Muslims live in America. The number of

mosques has doubled in the past twenty years, from 600 to 1200. About 135,000 Americans become Muslims each year, including about 35,000 annually from the prison population alone.[11] What does this say to the church?

Jesus Christ did not die at Calvary two millennia ago for white, middle-class Americans. He died for *people*—Muslims, Buddhists, atheists, Marxists, Mormons, and Unitarians. One of the ways Satan has blinded the minds of unbelievers (2 Cor. 4:4) is through false religious systems. In our politically correct and multicultural nation, the notion that Jesus offers the *only* way to God strikes many as intolerant, perhaps even bigoted. Still, God has spoken and He has not stuttered. Jesus was—and remains—the only way to God (John 14:6).

Churches in America must ask themselves whether they can continue to call themselves churches if they are open only to people just like their current members—ethnically, socially, economically, or physically.

The Open and Searching Unchurched

Many who are radically unchurched are so because no one has ever told them the truth. Many stand ready to embrace Jesus, if only someone would recognize their need and explain to them what the Word of God says. This group is characterized in Thom Rainer's myth 1, namely, that most unchurched think and act like Anglo, middle-class suburbanites with no church background.[12] Never assume that *any* person who is unchurched is, therefore, uninterested in the gospel.

In 1997, I went on a mission trip to New Hampshire, one of the most unchurched states in America. I asked one woman, "What is the greatest need in your area?" Without hesitating, she said, "People around here need hope." I handed her a booklet entitled "Here's Hope" (now *that* got her attention). I shared Christ with her, leaving her with a New Testament. This woman admitted that, although in her forties, she had a total ignorance of the gospel. She did not receive Christ that day; but she demonstrated that many, yes *many*, are willing to hear the story of Jesus if we will but take the time to share it.

But at a time when many are searching for spiritual meaning, the church's influence is decreasing. Does any other institution in America have more visibility (witness the church steeples across our land) and yet less influence?

A Gallup Poll notes that in the past forty years, 42 percent to 44 percent of the U.S. population attended church on a regular basis. The figure dipped to 38 percent in 1997. Barna also reports that from 1994 to 1996 the numbers of those who regularly attended church dropped from 42 percent to 38 percent. In 1994, however, a University of Notre Dame study found that number to be 26.7 percent.[13]

The Up and Out Unchurched: Happy Pagans

Evangelist and apologist Ravi Zacharias uses the term *happy pagans* to refer to a small but significant group of unchurched adults. Who are they? They are intellectually resistant to the gospel. Typically well-educated and financially successful, they are, Zacharias observes, "wrapped up in the belief that this world and the success it affords are the greatest pursuits in life." He continues: "Life has been reduced to temporal pursuits disconnected from all other disciplines necessary for life to be meaningfully engaged."[14]

An example of a happy pagan is Margaret, whom I met on an airplane. Margaret's husband is a corporate attorney in Arizona. She was returning from a trip to Raleigh, North Carolina, to find flooring for the five-thousand-square-foot home they were building. Financially, socially, and educationally they had it all. Yet when we began talking about children and the concerns of raising kids in this culture, Margaret's comments revealed a deep insecurity concerning more important issues of life.

Zacharias, who dialogues with such individuals across the nation, notes what they miss: "They are specialists with a glaring weakness: They do not ask the questions of life itself." He adds this example: "At the Harvard forum, I established that the law of non-contradiction . . . must apply to reality. . . . When I did, the audience went silent for several minutes. They had simply not taken time to see the inconsistencies of their lives. Zacharias offers a telling example:

> At Ohio State University, I did an open forum on a radio talk show. . . . One angry woman caller said, "All you people have is an agenda you're trying to promote." Referring to abortion, she said, "You want to . . . invade our private lives."
> Abortion had not even been brought up.
> "Just a minute," I replied. "We didn't even raise the subject."
> "What is your position on abortion then?"
> I said, "Can I ask you a question? On every university campus I visit, somebody stands up and says that God is an evil God to allow all this evil in our lives. . . ."
> I continued, "But when we play God and determine whether a child within a mother's womb should live, we argue for that as a moral right. So when human beings are given the privilege of playing God, it's called a moral right. When God plays God, we call it an immoral act. Can you justify this to me?"

That was the end of the conversation.[15]

Zacharias continues, "That the laws of logic apply to reality floors people, even though they use logic to attack Christian truths.

"Here's the rub: While the average secular person will believe something *without* subjecting it to rational critique, he disbelieves things on the basis that, he or she says, they are rationally inadmissible. So he critically attacks Christian assumptions using principles of logic that he doesn't even hold to."[16] In other words, the intellectualism of happy pagans lacks integrity; they will not consistently critique their own views in the same way they criticize the Christian faith.

A few years back a group of students at Southeastern Seminary became burdened for the unchurched in the area around the school. With the blessing of the faculty and administration, the group *doulos* (Greek for "bondservant") was born. Since that time, from thirty to over one

hundred students meet on Friday nights to share Christ in and around
Wake Forest. And every year since, the students knock on every door
and reach out to every neighborhood in the area.

Students and faculty have developed interesting perspectives on the
community. In particular, the most uninterested, hardest people are often the wealthiest. People who live in $800,000 homes seem to have all
they need, and God becomes an unwelcome intruder into their lifestyles.
But Jesus died for the hard-to-reach, up-and-out crowd also. Witnessing
to individuals who think that life is their oyster often includes the raising of questions, the sowing of a seed of doubt in their minds.

Zacharias and Frank Harber are two examples of apologists who effectively contend for the faith among the happy pagans.

_____

See Frank Harber's Web site at
www.defendingthefaith.com.

_____

The happy pagan is similar, too, to the people profiled in Lee Strobel's
book *Inside the Mind of Unreached Harry and Mary.* In his book, Strobel
describes various people, all of whom he calls Harry and Mary, from
suburban Chicago:[17]

- Harry teaches science in a local high school. He thinks that all
  religion is for intellectual weaklings.
- Mary is the extroverted neighbor who is perfectly happy without
  God in her life.
- Harry is the foreman at the construction site who uses Jesus'
  name as a swear word.
- Mary is so busy dealing with her success as an entrepreneur that
  she doesn't have time for spiritual matters.
- Harry is the businessman who shies away from Christianity be-
  cause he's afraid it might cramp the way he conducts his business.
- Mary is the university student whose experiences with her dad
  poisoned her attitude toward the idea of a heavenly father.

Strobel also gives sticking points that cause the unchurched to resist the faith:
1. I cannot believe. Reasons included science, suffering, dealing with evidence, etc.
2. I don't want to believe. It's a matter of the will.
3. I don't know what to believe.
4. I do believe; isn't that enough?
5. I don't want to believe what they believe.

One must understand that these happy pagans described by Zacharias and Strobel do not represent all the radically unchurched in America. They represent the upwardly mobile, generally well-educated adults who simply are too busy or too content with the things of the world to take seriously a relationship with God. Yet at some point they, too, realize their need for God; and the church has a mission to reach them as well.

Reaching the Radically Unchurched

As stated, the three groups described above by no means represent all the radically unchurched. While reading this, you've probably thought of some other people who fit the category; perhaps your eyes have been opened to the fields that teem with the unchurched. And the increasing numbers of radically unchurched are largely a result of the shift from modernism to postmodernism. Chapter four discusses this phenomena in more detail. At this point, it is important to stress that not all radically unchurched are postmodern, although virtually all postmoderns are unchurched.

This book encourages and equips you to reach the unchurched who live around you. But how can the church reach the radically unchurched? Through a radical commitment to Christ! Remember, the reason we must reach the unchurched is because that is what Jesus came to do and what He commissions us to do.

Jesus Serves as Our Model for Reaching the Unchurched

In every culture, among all peoples, at all times, the gospel answers the greatest human need. Survey the Gospels to see how our Lord responded to the lost world.

- His *Incarnation* demonstrated the very heart of God toward the ungodly. What a radical concept, that the Lord of Glory would abandon celestial security for a cruel cross.
- His *death and resurrection* demonstrate the lengths to which our Lord went to secure our redemption. Compared to the character of God we are all hopelessly lost. We deserve one thing—hell. Yet God has lavished His love on us through the cross.
- His *earthly ministry* demonstrates the ardor with which He sought the lost masses: His *accessibility* to people who are down and out, such as the Gaderene demoniac; His *being proactive* toward people, as in His approach to that social pariah the tax collector Matthew; His concern for an immoral, Samaritan woman. His ministry showed His *urgency* toward reaching people: "For the Son of Man has come to seek and to save that which was lost" (Luke 19:10 NKJV); "For even the Son of Man did not come to be served, but to serve, and to give His life a ransom for many" (Mark 10:45 NKJV). Finally, see the *hostility* of the religious hypocrites toward Jesus' love of lost people. "Friend of Sinners" became His moniker, and that not a complimentary one (Luke 7:34). Our Lord gave Himself to reach the world, and He has commissioned us to reach all people (Matt. 28:19–20), regardless of their spiritual background.

A History of Reaching the Radically Unchurched

God has on numerous occasions awakened His church to her need to live demonstrably changed lives and to penetrate the unchurched culture. In eighteenth-century England, the Anglican Church had become so institutionalized as to lack a passion for those outside the church. God used such servants as the Welsh layman Howell Harris, English evangelists John and Charles Wesley, and the young dynamo George

Whitefield to move outside the church walls to the people. They were not the first to preach in the fields, for our Lord modeled that in His ministry. But after no small amount of struggle these men moved outside their comfort zones in order to honor Christ. John Wesley, his brother Charles, along with Whitefield and others, faced much criticism for the seriousness with which they pursued the Lord. In college they and their peers were called the "Holy Club," "Bible Bigots," and other terms of derision. But God always has a place for such people. It was these men who faithfully preached salvation—whether in a church building or outside—through faith in Christ alone. Over time they preached more and more to the masses in the fields, although such a practice was not a comfortable one for them to embrace.

On February 17, 1739, Whitefield, aged twenty-four, preached for the first time outside the walls of a church to a group of miners in the fields. No one else cared for these rough colliers. His passion for God and his burden for those without Christ trumped his concern for his reputation.

> My bowels have long since yearned toward the poor colliers, who are very numerous, and as sheep having no shepherd. After dinner, therefore, I went upon a mount, and spake to as many people as came unto me. They were upwards of two hundred. Blessed be God that I have now broken the ice! I believe I was never more acceptable to my Master than when I was standing to teach those hearers in the open fields. Some may censure me; but if I thus pleased men, I should not be the servant of Christ.[18]

Similarly, John Wesley struggled with the idea of preaching outside. For a proper Anglican priest, educated at Oxford, such was quite out of the ordinary. Wesley even commented in his journal that until he preached in the fields, he had thought that one could be saved only in a church building.

That attitude plagues much of the church today. As we look at the masses of unchurched around us, may God give us a concern to reach those for whom Christ died rather than be satisfied with a cultural Christianity that focuses on fellowship and is devoid of the power of the gospel. Consider the compassionate heart of William Booth, the founder of the Salvation Army. Each Christmas, the churches in London sent representatives to the streets to invite the poor to a celebration. Thousands thronged there annually. Anglicans announced, "All of you who are Anglicans come with us." Catholics joined in, "All who are Catholics come with us." The Methodists, the Lutherans, and others followed suit. When all the invitations were made, many people still milled about. At that point, William Booth shouted to the people, "All of you who belong to no one come with me."[19] May God give us a generation of Christians with a heart for the unchurched like that of William Booth.

chapter two

A Vision for Reaching the World

What We Are Trying to Do

DEAN MET JESUS CHRIST in a life-changing way.

"Wonderful," you muse, "But hardly remarkable. After all, *everyone* who truly repents and believes meets Jesus in a life-changing way."

But Dean met Jesus in a life-changing way—while in jail.

"More remarkable," you shrug, "but still not so extraordinary."

But Dean met Jesus in a life-changing way while in jail, as he smoked the pages of Leviticus and read the gospel of John. Okay, *that* you don't see every day. In the early 1970s, this drug-abusing hippie and his live-in girlfriend were arrested in Mobile, Alabama. With no access to drugs in jail, Dean didn't even have a cigarette. He collected the cigarette butts left by other inmates, compacted the bits of tobacco he found, and frantically smoked the fragments.

Someone had left a Gideon Bible in Dean's cell. He noticed that the Bible had thin paper—great for rolling cigarettes! But as he rolled cigarettes with some of the pages, he found himself reading the Bible. By the inspiration of the Spirit of God, Dean figured out that, at this point in his life, John (with apologies to my colleagues in Old Testament studies) spoke more to him than did Leviticus. So he read John and smoked Leviticus. And, he got gloriously saved while incarcerated. Dean moved from being radically unchurched to radically saved. Today, you'll find Dean, a Southeastern Seminary graduate, serving God, sharing the gospel wherever he goes, winning people to Christ.

Which offends God more: A lost person like Dean using pages of the Bible for cigarettes, or a professing Christian who never reads God's Word?

Dean came from a totally unchurched background. He met Christ because someone put a Bible in a jail cell. It took a long time, though, for Dean and his girlfriend, who had also been saved while in jail, to join a local church. Was it because they refused to attend weekly services? No, it was because they had a difficult time finding a body of believers who would accept them just as they were, with their long hair and unsavory background. Increasing numbers of people in America are like Dean, except they still need to meet Jesus. Most, however, will not be reached solely by finding a Bible. Someone must tell them the Good News. When they find Jesus, can they find a church?

The Strategy Seen in Scripture

Who said these famous last words? "Give me liberty or give me death." Who said "I only regret that I have but one life to give for my country." These were the last words of Patrick Henry and Nathan Hale, respectively. Jesus Christ also left famous last words. In fact, the last thing Jesus said before He ascended into heaven contained both a promise and a command to His followers: "But you will receive power when the Holy Spirit comes on you; and you will be my witnesses in Jerusalem, and in all Judea and Samaria, and to the ends of the earth" (Acts 1:8 NIV). The promise of power and the command to witness guide the church to this day.

How the Church Relates to Culture

That the Lord compelled His followers to testify about Him is quite clear; there's no need to convince you of that. Evangelical believers throughout history have understood that, the *Great Commission* is not the *Great Suggestion*. The question is, how do we go about fulfilling that commission? How does our specific assignment to witness relate to the community of faith in general? These issues are summed up in one question: How does the church speak to culture? I'm indebted to Steve Sjogren for his analysis of the three ways in which the church typically relates to culture: evasion, pervasion, invasion.[1]

Evade

Some churches *evade* the culture. True, the Bible teaches that believers are to be separate from the world (1 Peter 2:9–10). And some liberal churches illustrate the pitfalls of ignoring the biblical mandate—it leads to an underemphasis on biblical doctrine, often in the name of relevance. Whether in regard to homosexuality or other areas of controversy, the church's desire to engage culture often leads to removing "outdated" biblical customs. But this response almost inevitably goes beyond customs, and affects theology and doctrine. The result is a church that looks just like the world and has thus lost any power to change it. Conservative churches, too, should look in the mirror; our emphasis on having an "abundant Christian life" is too often a cover for buying into materialism and self-gratification. We end up enjoying the pleasures of popular culture while trying to maintain a Christian identity, ignoring biblical ideals of sacrifice and the cost of discipleship.

While separation from worldliness is biblical, such truth does not contradict our Lord's command to impact culture with the gospel. Some churches want nothing to do with the world, including people for whom Jesus died. Most churches that evade the culture do so for one of two basic reasons. Some evade the culture out of fear—fear that worldliness will creep into the church, fear of the danger in the world. Such a desire to disengage from the world leads to a church that is like the monasteries of the Middle Ages—refuges for escaping from barbarians and barbaric views. It is interesting, however, that over a period of hundreds of years, the monastic movement could not remain introverted. Monastic movements began to reach out, becoming, in fact, outreach oriented, because the nature of the church is not to escape from the world but to reach the world with the gospel. Earnest, genuine believers who had joined a monastery in order to escape the world found themselves compelled to go into society to change it.

Another example of the fear mindset is seen in churches that become so polarized they, in some cases, forget that the gospel is for everyone. They don't want a black person, for example, coming into their church. Such churches are completely ineffective in reaching the unchurched. They refuse to saturate their community with the gospel because they may have to deal with a person from a totally different background in their community. Or they may need to take their Christianity out of the sanctuary and into reality. These are not neutral churches; rather, these churches hinder the work of God.

The second reason churches evade the world is because they simply don't care about the world. They're not interested in reaching the world because they're involved in such "important" issues as whether people should clap in church, or whether guitars violate Scripture, or whether the carpet should be green or brown. Such believers confuse their *preferences* with biblical *convictions,* and thereby become derailed on the way to obeying God. They are so sidetracked in discussing preferences that they fail to see the biblical conviction of penetrating the culture with the gospel.

We as believers should remain unstained from the world; we must not, however, be removed from the people for whom Christ died.

Pervade

A second way churches relate to culture is by seeking to *pervade* the world. These are the battlers, folks who seek to overpower the culture by might, be it political, social, or economic. They draw the line between the good guys and the bad guys, the churched and the unchurched. But, according to Ephesians 6, our fundamental battle is not between the unchurched and the churched; rather, it is between the forces of God and the forces of the Evil One. Churches that overemphasize the "pervade the world" mentality look more like political rallies than the body of Christ. (Incidentally, such churches can be on the far left, typically being liberal Democrats, or the far right, typically being conservative Republicans.) This group overemphasizes the role of political involvement to the neglect of the gospel.

It is time for the church to get out of the sanctuary and into reality.

It is not my intent to criticize those who are involved in politics, for we have a biblical responsibility to be civic minded. Rather, my plea is to maintain a focus on the gospel, giving priority to the power of the gospel over political persuasion. Spreading the gospel and being political doesn't have to be either/or; it is both/and. One needs, however, to maintain the proper priority.

Invade

A third way some churches relate to culture is by seeking to *invade* the world. Certainly the other two ways to relate, discussed above, contain a measure of merit. And while these approaches can be *good*, God seeks our *best*. And the best a church can be is to be like Jesus. *Jesus invaded the world through His Incarnation!* While we, like Jesus, should separate ourselves from sin, we should also influence our culture through the political realm; a biblical Christian is distinct from society and yet is a good citizen in it.

Which Best Describes Your Church?
- *Evade:* We must avoid the world at all costs.
- *Pervade:* We must overpower the world politically.
- *Invade:* We must penetrate the culture with the gospel.

God could have pervaded the world; He did, in fact, with the flood. But He did not give up on humanity. God certainly could have evaded the world, but the Word became flesh and invaded the world. Jesus left His home in glory, to come and live among us, to give us the opportunity to be a part of His kingdom. We, now, are the witness incarnate for Him until He returns. A church that follows the model of Jesus will be in the culture, among the people, making an impact for the gospel. Such a church invades the world, not to become like it but so that it would become like our Lord.

Note the sobering words of George McLeod:

> I simply argue that the cross should be raised at the center of the marketplace as well as on the steeple of the church. I am recovering the claim that Jesus was not crucified in a cathedral between two candles; but on a cross between two thieves on the town's garbage heap; at a crossroad so cosmopolitan they had to write His title in Hebrew and Latin and Greek . . . at the kind of place where cynics talk smut and thieves curse, and soldiers gamble. Because that is where He died and that is what He died about. That is where the churchmen ought to be and what churchmen ought to be about.[2]

The Power of God: What This World Needs

What will it take for the church to reach the unchurched? It will take more than a change of perspective. It will take more than desire, no matter how genuine, to be a church that invades the culture. It will take a church with the same radical abandonment to God as was seen in the early church. In the book of Acts, we read about the living, exciting, and supernatural New Testament church. These early believers faced danger, persecution, misinformation, and all manner of difficulties. Still, they thrived, reaching multitudes and growing rapidly.

Living the Christian life is not hard. It is *impossible* unless we live it by God's strength.

The church today also faces difficulties. Modern culture in the past few decades has lost respect and increased hostility for Christianity. Many in today's society see the church as a joke. And who can blame them? Television preachers talk about the power of God in one breath and beg for money in the next. Supposed faith healers parade themselves in the electronic media like the medicine men of a century ago. A friend of mine asked a well-known television faith healer, "If God gives you the power to heal, why do you refuse to visit patients in the hospitals?" After stuttering a bit, the preacher told my friend, "I don't feel led." Yet he feels led to take millions of dollars into his ministry (notice I said *his* ministry).

Don't misunderstand—God still does the miraculous. In fact, without the supernatural power of God, we will never reach this culture. Two points, though, are important. First, the greatest miracle is conversion, for in salvation a resurrection occurs (Eph. 2). Being resurrected is better than getting a new hand or receiving sight. Just ask the man born blind in John 9. Second, Scripture relates many miracles, but note—when did God perform a miracle? When He *needed to.* Miracles occurred in the book of Acts, and God still does them. But He does the miraculous when it is *needed,* not when a modern shaman dictates.

The problem in tapping into the power of God is twofold. First, some churches don't need the power of God, because they're built by using one creative scheme piled on top of another. They seek to affect culture by taking the philosophy, customs, and trappings of the world, and add a churchlike twist to them. The world doesn't need a church that resembles secular culture; it needs a people anointed by the hand of God. Second, others want the power of God, but only if they can use it at their disposal.

But God uses His power in His way, not in our way. And, as history demonstrates, His grace moves in supernatural power. In 1904–05, God stirred the little principality of Wales through the ministry of twenty-six-year-old Evan Roberts and others. Over 100,000 came to Christ in six months. Society was changed as well. Judges were presented with white gloves, which signified no cases needed to be tried. Alcoholism was cut in half. Miscreants made voluntary restitution. Gamblers, and others normally untouched by the ministry of the church, came to Christ.

Esteemed preacher G. Campbell Morgan recalled a conversation with a mine manager about profanity. The manager told him,

> The haulers are some of the very lowest. They have driven their horses by obscenity and kicks. Now they can hardly persuade their horses to start working, because there is no obscenity and no kicks.[3]

God so changed these miners that their own horses failed to recognize them!

The Bible, too, records the mighty work of God. Psalm 126 relates that, following the return of the Jews from the Babylonian exile, the nations around Jerusalem testified to the greatness of God. On several occasions in Acts, entire communities were filled with awe, or wonder, or even fear in response to God's activity among His people.

When I was a youngster, my church experienced what has become known as the Jesus Movement. During a short span in 1970, our small church in Birmingham, Alabama, witnessed the conversion of many hippie-types. We began a One Way Christian Night Club as a ministry. God changed many lives, including my own. Many today, including many leaders in churches, have never seen a mighty movement of God. We need a holy visitation, a God-intervention in our culture. God can do more during one week of revival in a church than we can accomplish through years of our feeble efforts alone.

The Need: Penetrating Culture with Gospel

In my lifetime, our culture has become ever darker. What was once taboo is now flaunted. The solution lies not in calling the darkness names, or griping about it, or throwing rocks. Our complaining about the lost world has been raised to an art form. The solution for darkness today is the same as in the past: turn on the light. The solution for coldness remains the same: turn up the heat.

The gospel—the good news about Jesus Christ, who is God, who became flesh, lived a sinless life, died in our place, rose from the dead, and stands ready to change the very destiny of those who repent—this gospel remains the answer. In the early 1970s, a popular saying in the Jesus Movement was "Jesus is the answer." On a poster displaying that slogan, some skeptic had written, "If Jesus is the answer, then what is the question?" Some young Jesus person wrote below the question, "It doesn't matter what the question is. Jesus is *still* the answer." Paul also reminds us in Romans 1 that the *gospel* is still the power of God to salvation.

The best way to get rid of the
darkness is simple: turn on the light!
The darkness of sin is forced out by
the gospel of light.

When addressing culture we begin with either the gospel or with people's needs. We choose to start with theology or anthropology. Most today begin with the needs of people. I believe we should begin with the Creator, not the creation; with the Savior, not those needing salvation. In other words, who better knows how to reach the lost world than the One who created the world?

John Avant, pastor of the New Hope Baptist Church in Fayetteville, Georgia, recounts a fascinating statistic. During a recent visit to Redondo Beach, California, Avant learned that 71 percent of that community had *never* entered a church building, not even for a wedding or funeral. Yet these same people reported that they were more spiritually hungry than at any previous time in their lives. Penetration of the culture with the message of the cross remains the task at hand.

History reverberates with examples of wondrous occurrences when the church remembered the power of the gospel. In 1949–50 Duncan Campbell ministered in the Hebrides Islands off the coast of Scotland. On one occasion he planned a two-week-long crusade. Following a season of intense prayer by the inhabitants of the Isle of Lewis, Campbell preached for the scheduled two weeks. No conversions were reported until the last day, when seven youths met Christ. When the benediction was given that night, a huge throng of people who had been teeming around the building pressed forward. Many more were saved, including

entire families. Campbell at last gave another benediction—at 2:00 A.M.!
The two-week-long crusade continued for two years! God had come,
and the gospel's power was obvious. On another occasion during that
period, a meeting that experienced the mighty presence of God continued until 4:00 A.M.

In the 1980s, I met a minister from Scotland. He said that some
thirty years later one could still sense the impact of the Hebrides Islands
Revival. How we need the power of the gospel to burn like a fire to reach
the unchurched.

> Jesus was criticized for being a
> friend of sinners (Luke 7:34).
> You will be more like Jesus based on the
> lost people you reach than the saved
> people you impress.

Stop reading for a minute; contemplate that the God who created the
universe, who remains far beyond our ability to comprehend, this only
true God owes us *nothing*—except hell. Despite this, He has lavished
His love on us through Christ. Such love should constrain us to reach a
lost world. Leonard Sweet makes an important distinction concerning
how we treat others. Noting that many today attempt to live by the
Golden Rule, Sweet asserts that Jesus gives His followers a higher goal:
"For Jesus, there was something beyond gold status. Jesus demanded
platinum discipleship. There is something beyond the golden rule, and
it is the platinum rule. We are to love one another as Christ loved us,
and how did He love us? He laid down His life for us."[4]

The Fuel: The Spirit

The Holy Spirit gives us our power. The reason we don't serve God in
power is that we fail to walk under the control of the Spirit. I love sports.
But, past forty and with an artificial hip, I'm not ready to take on the
NBA. Suppose I bought the best Air Jordan shoes, an authentic NBA

Vince Carter jersey, the coolest wristbands around, shaved my head, and got a tattoo? I'd still stink in comparison to the worst NBA player. Why? To use the vernacular, I've got no game. In America, our churches can have the finest buildings, the best resources, the latest version in Power Point presentations, praise teams that could win a Grammy award—but without the Spirit, we've got no game.

Imagine a group of believers so few in number they fit inside a small theater. They begin only with intent, passionately advancing into the world to preach Jesus to anyone who will listen. Their focus is not on their smallness but on God's greatness. Amazingly, many respond to the group. But not all respond positively. Thousands are saved, but community leaders determine that this Christian influence causes more harm than good. So they attempt to shut down the movement before too much momentum is gained. But these believers are different. They are fearless in the face of threats. Despite threats, imprisonment, and even the deaths of some of their leaders, the Christians continue to share the gospel, as if nothing mattered more to them than others hearing the Good News. At one point, they are charged with "turning the world upside down."

Does this band of believers operate in modern day Nepal? No, this is the story of the early church as recorded in the book of Acts. But there's more. These believers had no New Testaments or gospels of John to hand out. They had no gospel tracts. They had no denominational organization or a missions sending agency of which to speak. They had no training institutions, no Christian radio, and no (thank God, perhaps) Christian television. They had no ornate buildings. They had no freedom to vote. In fact, many were slaves.

These believers had none of the modern accoutrements of evangelizing. They had something better. That something was a Someone—the Holy Spirit of God. And so do you and I. Penetrating the darkness of an unchurched culture will take more than an occasional evangelistic blitz, although I believe in those. It will require the ongoing, intentional penetration of the unchurched world. Such an effort cannot be done by human strength. A century ago, Evan Roberts discovered the impact of the Spirit in Wales. As a young man, Roberts went to the front of a small church, knelt, and with great anguish cried, "Lord, *bend me.*" The Spirit of God filled him with power. Reflecting on that prayer, Roberts later recounted its effect: "I felt ablaze with a desire to go through the length and breadth of Wales to tell of my Savior; and had that been possible, I was willing to *pay* God for doing so."[5]

Make no mistake—without the work of the Spirit, we will not penetrate the unchurched culture. Without the Holy Spirit's control and power, we serve God in only our fleshly power. Sometimes God can even use that. As Spurgeon put it, God can hit good licks with crooked sticks. But this is not God's plan. When we walk in the fullness of the Spirit (Eph. 5:18), He becomes our trump card in the divine work of God. His wisdom can trump our ignorance; His compassion can trump our indifference; His boldness can trump our fears. Further, the Spirit can use all our efforts, no matter how feeble, to bring honor to the Father.

Jim's story could easily be that of many people in the United States. One would describe Jim as irreligious, indifferent to matters such as life after death or how the world will end. Jim didn't have time to think about a distant deity.[6] Jim's life reflected his upbringing; he was raised in a family committed to hard work, but not to church. He was taught how to look out for himself and for those he loved.

Jim's outlook underwent a slow change after he left home for college. His roommate during his freshman year was a guy named Andy. Andy was Jim's introduction to a way of life that he had never before encountered. Andy was a bona fide "Jesus Freak." He'd sing gospel songs in the shower (and he was LOUD), he'd turn on his desk lamp at 6 A.M. to read his Bible, he'd speak about spiritual subjects at almost every turn. The first week Jim met the young zealot, he didn't know what to think. But with time, Jim realized that Andy's irritating zeal was very genuine. Despite his bizarre practices, Andy loved with such admiration the Jesus about whom he spoke. It really affected Jim.

After his freshman year, Jim moved to an apartment, and during his latter years in college he joined a racket club. He was paired with Matt, a man just a few years his senior. Jim discovered that Matt was the youth pastor at the local evangelical church. By this time, Jim had questions about bigger concerns in life than where he would work after college. Matt helped him out, discussing with Jim how Jesus is the answer. This also got Jim's attention.

After graduation Jim took his first job. His secretary, Lori, personified professionalism. She also actively attended a local church. Each Monday she talked about the service from the day before. She had a little plaque on her desk that simply stated, "Prayer Changes Things." Her life demonstrated a belief in that statement. Lori never spoke badly about anyone, never complained, and was generally enjoyable to be around. Her attitude was rare and pleasant, and Jim noticed.

Eventually Jim married, witnessed the birth of his first son, and won a promotion at work. Jim's new boss, Bruce, was a hard-working man, and soon after transferring to his new position, Jim learned about an annual tradition in the office. Bruce invited Jim and all the office to his home for a cookout. At this cookout, Bruce shared his testimony of how Jesus Christ had changed his life and made all the difference in his work and family. Jim's own family was starting to have problems, and Jim noticed the difference between his family and Bruce's.

About a year later, Jim traveled across the country to a conference. At this point, he and his wife were having major problems in their marriage. On the airplane, Jim chatted with the lady sitting next to him. Jill was a good listener, and before long he had shared all his marital problems with her. "Jim," she finally replied, "Your marriage sounds much like mine. Just a few years ago, I didn't know how it would survive. But, one day, when we were at the end of our rope, someone told us about Jesus Christ and how He could change our lives. We committed ourselves to Him, and we've been changed. We certainly still had to work through our problems, and still are, but the Lord has been good to us." Her story made Jim do a great deal of thinking.

About two months later, Jim was home alone one night. While seated on the couch, watching a ball game, his doorbell rang. It was a witnessing team from the local evangelical church. Jim invited them in, and over the next half hour he heard the clear message of salvation from David, Stephanie, and Kathleen. By then Jim was ready. He knelt at his couch and yielded his life to Jesus.

Who led Jim to Jesus? Technically, the team of David, Stephanie, and Kathleen. But so did Andy, and Matt, and Lori, and Bruce, and Jill. Each had an impact on Jim. These believers simply followed Jesus' command in Matthew 4:19 to be fishers of men. The Holy Spirit, the Divine

Fisherman, used the gifts, abilities, and commitment of different believers. He wove each individual witness into a net that drew Jim into
the kingdom of God. As a result, Jim could also become a part of this
expanding net to reach the world with the gospel. You are a part of
God's net.

The Fire: Prayer

A man came home from work late—again—tired and irritated, to
find his five-year-old son waiting for him at the door.

"Daddy, may I ask you a question?"

"Sure, son, what is it?" replied the man.

"Daddy, how much money do you make an hour?"

"That's none of your business. What makes you ask such a thing?"
the man said angrily.

"I just want to know. Please tell me, how much do you make an
hour?" pleaded the little boy.

"If you must know, I make twenty dollars an hour."

"Oh," the little boy replied, head bowed. Looking up, he said, "Daddy,
may I borrow ten dollars please?"

The father was furious. "You want to know how much money I make
just so you can borrow some? You march straight to your room and go to
bed. Think about the way you're being so selfish. I work long, hard hours
every day, and I don't have time for such childish games."

The little boy shuffled to his room and shut the door. The man sat
down, getting even angrier about the little boy's questioning. *How dare
he ask such questions only to get some money?* After an hour or so, the man
had calmed down, and thought he may have been a little hard on his
son. Maybe he really needed that ten dollars and, after all, he didn't ask
for money often.

The man went to the boy's room and opened the door. "Are you
asleep son?" he asked.

"No, Daddy, I'm awake," replied the boy.

"I've been thinking, maybe I was too hard on you earlier," said the
man. "It's been a long day and I took my aggravation out on you. Here's
that ten dollars you asked for."

The little boy sat straight up, beaming. "Oh, thank you, Daddy," he yelled. Then, reaching under his pillow, he pulled out some more crumpled up bills.

The man, seeing that the boy already had money, started to get angry again. The little boy slowly counted out his money, and then looked up at his father.

"Why did you want more money if you already had some?" the father grumbled. "Because I didn't have enough, but now I do," the little boy replied. "Daddy, I have twenty dollars now. Can I buy an hour of your time?"

Children need time with their dads. But turn the story another way: How much time do you spend daily with God? And is the amount based upon how He provides? Many seek God for what He gives, and this is appropriate. But far better is seeking God simply to know Him. Prayer is intimacy with God, and if we are to reach unchurched people, it will begin not with evangelizing the lost, but with a relentless pursuit of the Lord.

Which of the following gets your best effort in a typical day? Rank from 1 to 5, 1 being highest, in order of priority to you:

_____ Eating

_____ Recreation

_____ Prayer and Bible Study

_____ Work

_____ Family Time

E. M. Bounds spoke prophetically, though not only to his generation: "What the church needs today is not . . . new methods, but men whom the Holy Ghost can use—men of prayer."[7] To restate Bounds, What the church needs today is not the latest trendsetting approach to youth ministry, or the best graphic designer to create a sermon with Power Point. What the church most needs today is men and women, and boys and girls, who have an insatiable appetite for God.

I've spoken in hundreds of churches across America, from tiny missions to massive megachurches. In every church I meet people who deeply love Jesus, who long to know Him more. But Allister McGrath raises an interesting point: "People need help with prayer, devotion, and personal discipline [and I would add, witnessing!]—and if evangelicalism is not providing it, is it really surprising that they may turn elsewhere?"[8]

Too many evangelical believers turn to television preachers who have questionable theology, books that foster New Age ideas more than biblical conviction, and common fiction over biblical truth. It is time for leaders in the church to do what Jesus did—teach people to pray.

Many Christians today decry that prayer has been taken out of public schools. That loss is a sad commentary on our society. More tragic, however, is that the *church* has forsaken prayer. Do we really have a right to criticize the absence of prayer in schools when we don't pray even in our homes? Or, for that matter, in our churches? But that's changing. A growing prayer movement is sweeping America. Fasting, once unheard of in many circles, has become a normal practice in churches across the land.

One of the most exciting examples of a church penetrating the unchurched culture is the Brooklyn Tabernacle in New York. Pastor Jim Cymbala has led the congregation to love the ungodly. This church has reached junkies, prostitutes, homosexuals, as well as lawyers and businessmen. Truly multiethnic, the Brooklyn Tabernacle is a hospital for the hurting.

The success of Brooklyn Tab lies in the prayer of God's saints there. Their world-famous choir sometimes spends half of rehearsal not singing, but praying. Back when the church began to grow, prayer dominated every aspect of ministry. When Sunday attendance reached 150 to 175, the Tuesday night prayer meeting numbered 100! Today, over 1500 meet weekly for the prayer meeting. Cymbala gives a main reason for the powerful prayer at Brooklyn Tab: "The roughness of inner-city life has *pressed* us to pray. When your teenagers are getting assaulted and knifed on the way to youth meetings, when you bump into a transvestite in the lobby after church, you can't escape your need for God."[9] The problem with many churches today is that they simply do not see the need to pray.

No need to pray? Across our cities violence is escalating, tragedies impact believers at Columbine High School and Wedgwood Baptist. Is it really okay anywhere? What will it take to drive us to our knees? What must God do to burden us for the lost around us?

In St. Louis, Missouri, I saw a poster that I've never forgotten. The pastor of a church there, Timothy Cowin, is a man with a passion for God. On the wall in his study is a picture given to Timothy by his wife, Jill. It pictures a man prostrate on the floor in prayer. The caption, in large letters, declares, "MAKE WAR ON THE FLOOR." The Scripture reference is 2 Corinthians 10:4. Penetrating our culture with the gospel begins with prayer. S. D. Gordon, a man of prayer, said, "We can do more than pray after we have prayed, but we cannot do more than pray until we have prayed."

Prayer—Intimacy with God that leads to the fulfillment of His purposes.

The goal of prayer is not merely to talk to God, or even to get answers. The goal of prayer is to know Him. I define prayer as intimacy with God that leads to the fulfillment of His purposes. Our desire in evangelism should be to bring more people into the kingdom to worship and know God. The issue is not whether we can reach an unchurched culture. The issue is whether we have prayed and obeyed. When we do, God does work. At a national conference, I heard about a church that tested the effectiveness of prayer. They identified eighty homes and prayed for those homes daily for ninety days. After the ninety days, witnessing teams were dispatched to these homes as well as to eighty other homes that had received no prayer support. Of the eighty homes that received no focused prayer, only one family invited them in for a visit. Of the eighty homes that received the ninety days of prayer, *sixty-seven* welcomed the teams! Prayer matters.

The Vessel: A Holy Life

Light and heat are distributed through vessels of some sort—a fireplace, a lantern, a light bulb. Each of us is God's vessel. Thus, the purity of our lives will allow the light and heat to reach those around us.

In the nineteenth century, pastor Robert Murray McCheyne preached the ordination message for a young deacon named Edward. He challenged Edward: "A holy man is an awesome weapon in the hand of God." A believer focused on holy living will be a mighty tool in the hand of God to reach this generation as well.

Our tendency as fallen people leads us to seek answers to dilemmas—even those of a spiritual nature—through our own ingenuity: do a demographic study, categorize those we seek to reach, and then draw up a strategy. It sounds so simple, so businesslike, so packaged. And it is so wrong—especially if that's all we do. The secret to reaching people today remains the same as always—the revealed truth of the gospel shared through our words and our lives.

Scripture teaches that any spiritual endeavor requires spiritual power. Witness Paul's reminder in Ephesians 6 that our struggle is with principalities and powers, not with New Agers and postmoderns. He tells us to put on the armor of God, a metaphor for the spiritual armament necessary to prevail against the dark forces from the demonic world.

Rachel Scott's parents know against whom they struggle. I sat in awe of this couple as they were interviewed only days after their daughter's martyrdom at Columbine. "Can you forgive the killers?" they were asked. "We never blamed them, so we do not need to forgive them," was the reply. Then Rachel's mother said, "The reason this happened is because of the evil one [Satan], not two boys."

The question confronting the church today is, Are we *assaulting* the kingdom of darkness? Consider this personal question: Are you known in hell? If you're a believer, you'll find your name in the Lamb's book of life. So you are known in heaven. But, are you known in hell? Acts 19 relates an interesting incident. Seven Jews, sons of a man named Sceva, try to expel a demon in the name of Jesus and Paul. The demon speaks: "Jesus I know, and Paul," he retorts, "But who are you?"

The question implied in this New Testament passage is not whether we can identify demons, but whether they can identify us. Luke reported that the evil spirits knew Paul on a first name basis. It would be a sad thing, then, if a Christian was unknown in hell. Let's say your name is

John. Would it not be more honoring to Christ if, when you awaken in the morning, some demon cried out, "OHHHHHHH NOOOOOO!! JOHN IS AWAKE!!! LOOK OUT!!" Maybe if our lives more reflected the light of the gospel, the residents of hell would take notice.

How do we assault the kingdom of Satan? How do we invade the kingdom of darkness? We do it by air, by land, and by sea (at least by analogy). By air, we call upon the might of God through prayer. By sea, the Holy Spirit fills us and God's Word acts like a naval blockade, stopping the flow of evil. On land, we launch an invasion, going person to person, presenting the glorious gospel. But all this flows through the channel of a holy life.

McGrath asserts that when the Reformation came in the sixteenth century, the spiritual life it produced stood in stark contrast to the monasticism of prior times: "With the Reformation the formative centers of spirituality gradually shifted from the monasteries to the marketplace, as the great cities of Europe became the cradle and crucible of new ways of Christians thinking and acting."[10] We need a similar shift of focus in relating our faith to the culture today. We need to get out from behind the cloistered walls of our churches and into the community. Across America, God is raising up a generation of Christians who are sick and tired of being sick and tired—sick that God is being banished from the minds and hearts of America, tired of just sitting by and watching it happen. They sense a stirring, a movement of God's Spirit, compelling them to do more than mark time until Jesus comes. Does this describe you? Then read on. Because what the *world* needs today is exactly what the world needed in the first century—believers who can be described like this:

> Now when they saw the boldness of Peter and John, and perceived that they were uneducated and untrained men, they marveled. And they realized that they had been with Jesus.
> —Acts 4:13 NKJV

chapter three

The Power of One

The Reason You Live

SEPTEMBER 15, 1999, seemed like a typical day in my evangelism class. As we took prayer requests at the beginning of class, I posed the question that I posed in the last chapter: "What will it take to awaken the church to its need to penetrate the culture with the gospel? Must someone come into a church during worship, guns blazing, before we realize that God is trying to awaken the church?" I posed the question rhetorically, or so I thought. That evening my rhetoric became reality. As Michelle and I watched the news about hurricane Floyd in North Carolina, a reporter announced a shooting in a Fort Worth church. We were shocked to learn it was the Wedgwood Baptist Church, where we had been members in the 1980s when I attended seminary.

The tragedy of Wedgwood illustrates the reality of Romans 8:28 (NKJV): "And we know that all things work together for good to those who love God, to those who are the called according to His purpose." Out of the darkness, God's light still shines, especially in the life of a teenager named Jeremiah Neitz.[1] As the mentally disturbed Larry Gene Ashbrook entered the church, Neitz courageously faced him. Neitz was part of a youth group at South Wayside Baptist Church who were attending a See-You-at-the-Pole Rally at Wedgwood Baptist. Jeremiah and another young man sat with their youth pastor, Adam Hammonds, near the back of the church. As the music of a band played, shots were fired. "Adam and I were going to walk out to see what was going on and the glass shattered in the doors," Neitz recalled. "We ran and yelled 'Get down! Get down!' and got down in our seats." Two had been killed and three wounded by the time Ashbrook, a loner and lunatic, walked into the auditorium.

As he fired his gun around the room, people prayed and ducked for cover. Jeremiah sat up in the pew and prayed with hands folded. Ashbrook seemed irritated at this; his shooting rampage, which killed five more, did not cause all his hostages to cower in fear. He cursed and decried their faith, shouting, "Your religion [expletive]." Jeremiah could not keep silent. "No, sir, it doesn't," he said as he turned to face the gunman.

"Yes it does!" cried a more irritated Ashbrook.

"No, sir, it doesn't."

Jeremiah Neitz stood facing Larry Gene Ashbrook hardly a pew-length away. "What you need is Jesus Christ," Neitz said. The youth's words seemed to confuse the gunman. He slumped into a pew at the rear of the sanctuary, with what witnesses described as a look of disbelief on his face. As Ashbrook sat, Jeremiah stood. Pastor Hammond tugged at Jeremiah's leg, trying to get him to take cover. Trey Herweck, a twenty-four-year-old seminary student, said Jeremiah looked fearless as he faced Ashbrook. Ashbrook aimed the gun at Jeremiah's head. "Sir," Neitz said, "you can shoot me if you want. I know where I'm going—I'm going to heaven." Hammond thought this would only enrage the gunman, provoking him to fire. A shot was fired—Hammond thought this signaled the death of Neitz. Instead, Ashbrook had put the gun to his own head, taking his life.

One person, and that person a youth only recently returned to God, stopped the killing.

I won't ask whether you would have responded like Neitz. The answer is merely hypothetical unless we're facing a gun barrel. The more pressing question is, Are you and I living a life abandoned to the purposes of God?

The Power of One Person

September 11, 2001, will never be forgotten by those living in the United States on that day. I was preparing to go to chapel on our campus when I heard of the terrorist attacks on the World Trade Center and the Pentagon. An incredible toll in human lives was taken that day, and not a single "weapon," in the traditional sense of the term, was used.

Behind the suicidal fanatics and the strategists and planners of the attacks was the leadership of Osama bin Ladin. Bin Ladin has no official political portfolio beyond the personal fortune he gives lavishly to advance his cause. Yet it is this one man's ability to command the hatred, loyalty, and energy of others that changed the world on a single day. How much can God do through a believer who is willing to pay the price to make a difference?

Our earth has more than six billion inhabitants. With such a crowd, one may be tempted to doubt the value of one baby or another. One might develop the attitude that not everyone really matters. Consider the following scenarios:

1. A minister and his wife, who live in extremely modest conditions, discover they are expecting their fifteenth child. Considering their poverty and the excessive world population, is this baby needed?
2. A young man is victim to a number of serious health problems, and his wife has tuberculosis. Of their four children, one is blind, one has died, one is deaf, and one has tuberculosis. Now the woman finds that she is pregnant again. Surely this is an unneeded baby, is it not?
3. As the result of rape by a white man, a thirteen-year-old black girl is pregnant. If you were her parents, would you recommend that she endure the risky and emotionally traumatic pregnancy to bring the child of a rapist into the world?
4. In the midst of a society where sexual propriety is regarded as essential, a teenage girl is pregnant. Her betrothed knows that he is not the father of the baby, and he will share in her condemnation if he does not reject her. Does the world need this baby?

Each of these situations falls within the quality of life categories in which people many would find abortion to be appropriate. However, if you believe abortion would be an acceptable option in the first case, you have justified the death of John Wesley, who will become one of the great evangelists of the eighteenth century. In the second case, you have opted to deprive the world of composer Ludwig von Beethoven. In the third case, you have discarded Ethel Waters, who will inspire millions as a gospel musician. In the fourth scenario, of course, you have voted for the murder of Jesus Christ.[2]

These are atypical examples, particularly in the divinely orchestrated birth of Jesus. Still, according to the Word of God, every single individual is worth the death of Jesus. Therefore, every person from Jeremiah—who was told that God already had plans for him when he was still in his mother's womb—to Paul, to *you,* has a vital role to play in the economy of God.

Maybe now you're thinking, "Yes, I understand that people matter. And for the unchurched population, the gospel matters. And I realize that life is a lot different than it was in the fifties. We must go after the unchurched. But what does this have to do with me?"

Do you remember where you were and what you were doing when you heard about the events of September 11, 2001? Do you remember how you felt? I was stunned. Those whose own lives and relationships collapsed on that day may struggle in vain to make some sense of what happened. Others of us just throw our hands up in despairing surrender, asking, "This is horrible, but what can we do?" In response to such incidents, outrage and inspired vision soon wither to exhausted helplessness. We have a wrong perspective. You cannot change the whole world. People of great moral and political influence are unable—alone—to change the course of a culture. But God never called you or me as individuals to change the whole world. You'll only give up in frustration if you try. God called us to change *our part* of His world. And you can only truly live by seeking, through the grace of God, to change *your* world. Make the world different where you live.

God has not called you to change the whole world. He has called you to change *your* world through His strength.

Such is the legacy of Rachel Scott. While events surrounding Rachel's murder at Columbine High School in Colorado may never be perfectly known, she represents the stand taken by Christians in the face of death that day. She is one of the most influential Christians from 1999. I would argue, in fact, that the most influential Christians in America the last year of the second millennium A.D. were teenagers killed at Columbine on August 20, 1999, and the high school and seminary students killed at Wedgwood Baptist Church in Fort Worth, Texas, on September 15, 1999.

An entry in Rachel's journal dated April 20, 1998—one year to the day before her murder at the hands of two Columbine High School classmates—reveals a teenager lamenting her plight. Rachel was far from a "super Christian." She struggled as a Christian, especially with losing close friends when she wouldn't yield to peer pressure.

"I lost all of my friends at school," one entry recorded. "Now that I have begun to 'walk my talk,' they make fun of me. I don't even know what I have done. I don't really have to say anything, and they turn me away.

"I know what they're thinking every time I make a decision to resist temptation and follow God. They talk behind my back and call me 'the preacher's church-going girl.'" She had lost five of her closest friends in the previous six months. The first friend had gone from a sweet "preppie" to a trench-coat-wearing pot smoker. "I am not going to justify my faith to them, and I am not going to hide the light that God has put into me," she wrote. "If I have to sacrifice everything, I will. I will take it. If my friends have to become my enemies for me to be with my best friend Jesus, then that's fine with me. I always knew that being a Christian is having enemies, but I never thought that my 'friends' were going to be those enemies."[3]

But what most impressed Rachel's youth minister was her passion: "She had a passion for God and a passion for people. . . . She loved them and wanted them to know Christ. I was just amazed by the strength she had to stand out." Rachel's legacy is a great one, not because she set out to make a name for herself, but because she had a passion for Him.

The *Times* of London recommended
"10 trends for 1999." One of these was
"an audience of one." It observed that
consumers in our day crave individually
tailored products. This only reflects the biblical
position that each of us receives individual
attention from our Creator.

As a preteen I was an insecure, skinny, introverted little boy. How could God use me? Some days I felt like a balloon with the skin peeled off—a big nothing! But as I entered high school, more and more adults began to challenge me: "Alvin, you can make a difference for Jesus if you will!" I read about people like Samuel Mills, who as a college student proposed to his buddies that they should reach Asia with the gospel. He challenged them, saying, "We can do it if we will!" Out of that group came not only Mills, but also Adoniram Judson and Luther Rice.

No, you can't change the whole world. But what about *your* world? Through the power of God's Spirit, change as much of *your* world as you can. Who lives in your world? Who are other believers you can challenge to abandon themselves to God? Who are unchurched people you can befriend, and get to know, and seek to reach for the sake of Jesus?

In just a few decades, a little gaggle of Galileans, a band of believers, *turned their world upside down.* Our world is upside down from sin. Only the Lord can turn it back over again. And God will do this through us. If every believer—no, if half the believers—no, if *ten percent* of believers in America genuinely sought to change their world, in a decade we would live in a different country. Will you take the challenge? Will you do your part?

Perhaps you're thinking, *What do I have to offer God?* I meet people all the time who emphasize what they can*not* do to the glory of God. "I can't teach, I can't sing, I'm shy." My reply is a Greek word for such excuses: *baloney.*

Remember others God has used:

- A stuttering, often cowardly man killed someone, yet God made Moses the greatest leader in Israel's early history.
- The least in his family, this youngster was overlooked even by godly Samuel, but God made him king David. Acts 13:36 says, "When David had served God's purpose in his own generation . . ." (NIV) David shows us what happens when one—just *one*—served the Lord in his generation. God's purpose for you may not be to lead a nation; but His purpose does include serving the Lord in your generation. If you do serve Him, you'll probably make a greater impact than you can imagine. The Greek word translated "serve" means an "under-rower," one chained to the oars in the hull of a ship, whose life is consumed with rowing. Be consumed with serving the Lord, and watch how He uses you!
- A profane, rough fisherman became Peter an apostle. Even if you sometimes stumble over your words or say dumb things, God can still use you.
- A geek with more brainpower than ten normal people, Jonathan Edwards was powerfully used of God in the First Great Awakening in America.
- John Wesley, a scrawny little fellow, was used as a tool of great revival in England.
- A tall, thin man was told by one college president that he would never be a great preacher, but look how God used Billy Graham.
- And recently, God used the deaths of a couple of teenaged young ladies in Littleton, Colorado, to awaken a nation.

God may not give you the same range of influence that these people have had. But He used a Sunday school teacher named Edward Kimble to win to Christ the great evangelist D. L. Moody. Oh, friend, let God use you. Don't sit around begging God to use you, get to work for Him—and He will use you up!

A big chunk of iron in a horseshoe factory can be used to make maybe $50 worth of horseshoes. The same chunk of iron can be used to produce $500 worth of fine ink pens. But the same chunk of iron in the Silicon Valley can be used to make semiconductors worth $500,000! It all depends on who molds the iron. If you live solely in your own power, seeking your desires, your life is no more useful to God than a pile of horseshoes. If you serve the Lord but still seek to control your overall destiny, you—like a nice pen—have some usefulness, may serve some utilitarian use for the kingdom. But if you abandon yourself totally to God's purpose, He will mold you into a vessel that communicates a message more powerfully than does the greatest computer on earth.

God doesn't use *somebodies;*
He uses *nobodies* full of Him!
—Evangelist Bill Stafford

God has planted in you and in everyone a vision to live for Him. He has made you with a sense that there is something you *must* do. This process starts at conversion, but it only starts there. Your vision grows as you passionately follow Jesus. When a passion for God drives you to find His vision, you begin the process of learning His purpose for you. As a result, you experience the great adventure of the Christian life.

A few words of caution. First, in seeking God's vision—that is, His big picture for you—seek to know *Him* more than His *vision.* A second class Christian only wants enough of God to have security in His will. A first class Christian seeks to know *Him.* More than to provide a roadmap for you, God desires to have a growing relationship with you.

Second, in pursuing God's purpose (the daily working out of His will), God's Word guides. He will never lead you contrary to His Word. Too many today get excited about Jesus, begin to experience a touch from Him, and then waste their lives pursuing self-serving experiences in the name of honoring Him. If God reveals His will, it will be consistent with the Great Commission and the Great Commandment, as well as the entirety of His revealed Word. He will not lead you away from the church, away from integrity, away from obedience.

Third, let your passion be above all else for Him. Let the reason you live be a relentless pursuit of God. Above all else, pursue Him. If you do, you will be driven to make an impact among the unchurched around you, for you will share the passion of your Lord to seek and save the lost.

Your Church: The Power of One Body

One person alone will never change the whole world. And focusing too much on individualism goes against Scripture. Each believer is to be part of a community of faith called a "church." That is how to change the world.

I love my church. It's far from perfect, because it has members like *me*. But in its second decade of existence, Faith Baptist Church has one thing going for it. We love unchurched people. At our church can be found guys with earrings (and people of either gender with other assorted body piercings and art). There are all kinds of hair styles. Our motivation to reach out is based on need rather than appearance. With that philosophy we have grown from a handful to nearly two thousand in weekly attendance. Our church has recaptured the mission of the church to reach the unchurched of the world.

American society teems with millions who seek community. They search in many venues—at bars or nightclubs, through political or charitable causes, and recently, in thousands of Internet chat rooms or online virtual cities. Among the youth population, gangs have become the alternative to the family. Yet the church that honors Jesus offers the greatest and most important community, and it is available to all.

Sweet asks a pointed question of churches: "In a 24–7–365 world, how many churches are still 1–1–52 (1 hour, 1 day a week, 52 weeks a year)?"[4] In other words, we must be doing ministry 24 hours a day, 365 days a year. Believers must have the same passion at their jobs on Monday that they exhibit singing in church on Sunday. The inconsistency of church members is a major hindrance to reaching the unchurched.

The early church had no such thing as Sunday-only Christianity. It had simply Christianity, and it pervaded every second and every aspect of their lives. We must recapture the biblical notion that people, not buildings, comprise the church. On Sunday, the church is gathered. On Monday, that same church is scattered. We must break free from the isolation and stagnation found in so many congregations. Archbishop William Temple said the Church of England was so "proper" that she was in danger of dying of good taste. So may the entire organized church in our day. As Sweet puts it, "Some of us need to be converted away from Christianity,"[5] that is, the cultural Christianity of our day. Many today seem to take out a plastic, inflatable Jesus and take Him—along with their Sunday clothes, and Sunday Bibles, and Sunday-only Christianity—to church. Such a plastic Jesus will not make an impact on anyone. Such a plastic Jesus scandalizes our Lord.

The church is a community of faith bound together to obey the Lord. In an age increasingly hostile to the Christian faith, the church can make a profound impact not by compromising to the world's tastes, but by providing genuine community, something increasingly lacking in our fragmented culture. Organizations with vibrant small groups continue to flourish while institutions living on tradition are declining.

"For example," Sweet has observed, "old centers of power are declining: the PTA, the Red Cross, the League of Woman Voters, the Boy Scouts are barely surviving. JAYCEES have lost 44 percent of members since 1979, and the Masons are down 30 percent since 1959. The only reason Kiwanis clubs have not gone that way is they have added women to their membership. Since 1983, the Elks are down 21 percent, and the Lions are down 12 percent. Labor Unions are also in decline. But new groups like Promise Keepers have exploded; and the most tremendous growth has come online in chat groups, online communities which people log-on to by the millions to find their sense of community."[6]

Did You Know?
Did you know the founders of MTV did not seek simply to create a music video network, but to produce a culture? We have forgotten that Christianity is not simply adherence to a creed, but an entire culture, which should permeate and thus affect every aspect of life. Is your church trying to change your culture?

It is to our shame that at a time when so many long to belong, they turn to chat rooms on the Internet because no church cares for them. The Web has, in fact, become for this generation what the front porch was in by-gone days. Some groups have even created cyber-churches, which only encourage isolation from real relationships in the name of innovative Christianity. Can the church build the kind of community that draws the hurting to her?

After a speech, an old man approached Pro-Life activist Penny Lea. Weeping, he told her the following story:

> I lived in Germany during the Nazi holocaust. I considered myself a Christian. I attended church since I was a small boy. We had heard the stories of what was happening to the Jews, but like most people today in this country, we tried to distance ourselves from the reality of what was really taking place. What could anyone do to stop it?
>
> A railroad track ran behind our small church, and each Sunday morning we would hear the whistle from a distance and then the clacking of the wheels moving over the track. We became disturbed when one Sunday we noticed cries coming from the train as it passed by. We grimly realized that the train was carrying Jews. They were like cattle in those cars!
>
> Week after week that train whistle would blow. We would dread to hear the sound of those old wheels because we knew that the Jews would begin to cry out to us as they passed our church. It was so terribly disturbing! We could do nothing to help these poor miserable people, yet their screams tormented us. We knew exactly at what time that whistle would blow, and we decided the only way to keep from being so disturbed by the cries was to start singing our hymns. By the time that train came rumbling past the churchyard, we were singing at the top of our voices. If some of the screams reached our ears, we'd just sing a little louder until we could hear them no more. Years have passed and no one talks about it much anymore, but I still hear that train whistle in my sleep. I can still hear them crying out for help. God forgive all of us who called ourselves Christians, yet did nothing to intervene.
>
> Now, so many years later, I see it happening all over again in America. God forgive you as Americans for you have blocked

out the screams of millions of your own children. The holocaust is here. The response is the same as it was in my country—*silence!*[7]

While Lea applied this holocaust story to the millions of abortions
performed in America, it also speaks to the negligence of the church in
seeking to save lost souls from hell. May our generation not be so busy
spending time in activity that we miss the cries of the hurting. Tell someone about Jesus, won't you?

The Crisis of Busyness and the Need to Belong

Satan called a worldwide convention. In his opening address to his
evil angels he said, "We can't keep the Christians from going to church.
We can't keep them from reading their Bibles and knowing the truth.
We can't even keep them from conservative values. But we can do something else. We can keep them from forming an intimate, abiding relationship with Christ. If they gain that connection with Jesus, our power
over them is broken. So let them go to church, let them have their conservative lifestyles, but steal their time, so they can't maintain that connection with Jesus Christ.

"How shall we do this?" shouted his angels.

"Keep them busy in the nonessentials of life and invent distractions
to occupy their minds," he answered. "Tempt them to spend, spend,
spend, then borrow, borrow, borrow. Persuade the wives to go to work
for long hours and the husbands to work six or seven days a week, ten to
twelve hours a day, so they can afford their lifestyles. Keep them from
spending time with their children. As their family fragments, soon their
homes will offer no escape from the pressures of work.

"Over stimulate their minds so that they cannot hear that still small
voice. Entice them to play the radio or cassette player whenever they
drive, to keep the TV, VCR, CDs and their PCs going constantly in
their homes. And see to it that every store and restaurant in the world
constantly plays non-biblical music with contradicting messages. This
will jam their minds and break that union with Christ.

"Fill their coffee tables with magazines and newspapers. Pound their minds with the news twenty-four hours a day. Invade their driving moments with billboards. Flood their mailboxes with junk mail, sweepstakes, mail order catalogs, and every kind of newsletter and promotional offering free products, services, and false hopes.

"Even in their recreation, let them be excessive. Have them return from their recreation exhausted, disquieted, and unprepared for the coming week. Don't let them go out in nature to reflect on God's wonders. Send them to amusement parks, sporting events, concerts, and movies instead.

"And when they meet for spiritual fellowship, involve them in gossip and small talk so that they leave with troubled consciences and unsettled emotions. Let them be involved in soul-winning. But crowd their lives with so many good causes they have no time to seek power from Christ. Soon they will be working in their own strength, sacrificing their health and family for the good of the cause."

It was quite a convention. And the evil angels went eagerly to their assignments, causing Christians everywhere to get busy, busy, busy and rush here and there. Has the Devil been successful at his scheme? You be the judge.

If Satan can't make you bad, he'll keep you busy.

Faith Popcorn, a futurist who closely watches popular culture, reflects on our busy lives. "We don't want more anything anymore," She writes. "What we want now is less, more and more less. Most of us never tape TV shows because (1) it means we have to crack the secret agent instruction manual code, (2) we have to learn to program the VCR, and (3) we don't have time to watch the taped shows anyway."[8]

The church as a community can demonstrate how Christianity affects daily living. When our priorities are right, the world sees the practical ways in which following Jesus helps us to survive in a culture of busyness. But the church needs first to evaluate her priorities. If church leaders did two things, it would make an incredible impact on our ability to reach the lost. First, help church members to slow down their lives in this culture that is running people ragged. Busyness competes with materialism as one of the great sins of the American church. Even in the church, so many are so tired from doing so many things that have so little of eternal value to show for their efforts. Busyness is *not* a spiritual gift!

Second, and most vital, we must take churches back to their essential purpose. Foundational to reaching the radically unchurched is a serious retooling of the church. Far too many have lost the purpose of the church. My specific prayer is that God will raise up a new generation of church leaders—pastors, staff members, and church planters—who won't settle for the maintenance mentality found in so many churches. One of our goals at Southeastern Baptist Theological Seminary is to take every student on an overseas mission trip. This will expand the horizons of these future leaders and help give them a broken heart for a lost world.

The resources listed below, while written from a variety of perspectives, all say essentially the same thing about the purpose of the church. Read these three over a brief period and note their points in common. Then, take your people to the New Testament and teach them what the church is to be about. It may take a few years to turn some churches; but it is worth the journey.
- Mims, Gene. *Kingdom Principles for Church Growth*. Nashville: Convention Press, 1995.
- Robinson, Darrell. *Total Church Life*. Nashville: Broadman and Holman, 1996.
- Warren, Rick. *The Purpose-Driven Church*. Grand Rapids: Zondervan, 1995.

Thom Rainer's myth 2 (see pg. 25) about the unchurched is that they loathe denominational names like *Baptist* or *Methodist*.[9] A name doesn't turn off the unchurched. What makes the unchurched uninterested is the failure of believers to live what we profess. If any word demonstrates what the lost need to see in your church, it's the word *real.* Televangelism scandals and lifeless churches cause multitudes to question the reality of the message of the church. More than a miracle show, or contemporary music, or the latest in technology, people long for what is real. Consider the popularity of so-called "reality TV," shows like *Survivor.* What viewers do not understand is that these are not actually "real." Real means experiencing life as God intends. Rainer's myth 5 states that, in order to reach the unchurched, the pastor must be dynamic and have a charismatic personality.[10] No—more than ability, lost people seek individuals who are real.

All Believers in the U.S.:
The Power of One People of God United

We must not look at the present darkness as did Elijah after his encounter with the prophets of Baal at Mount Carmel. The great prophet felt that he was the only person who stood for God. But the Lord reminded him of seven thousand who stood for God. True, there is much darkness in our culture. But God remains on the throne. Peter Steinfels argues that not only is evangelicalism alive and well, "it appears to be the strongest of the major Christian traditions in the United States today."[11]

I travel to about twenty or more states every year. I speak in big cities and small towns, in the Bible Belt and far beyond the southeast. Yet, everywhere I go, I see evidence of Christian life. It may be a WWJD bracelet on a teen, or Christian T-shirts worn by a family, or a sister in Jesus I meet in attempting to witness. But one thing is certain, if you look for a Christian, you'll soon find one. Yes, we are in the minority in this culture, but we are not absent.

And motivated by a united purpose we could make a huge impact on modern culture. How? Do you know why movies become popular? A well-known actor helps, as do special effects and ad campaigns. But some movies, even with all the above, still bust—while others without these elements become sleeper hits. The reason is simple: word of mouth. A good movie excites those watching it. What if every Christian in America woke up one day and, realizing the complete and radical significance

Jesus had made in his or her life, became radical, fanatical, and unashamed to tell others about the change Jesus made? The word of mouth testimony from all these believers would make the headlines!

Example: What We *Could* Do

Here's one example of how we, as one body, could radically affect culture across America.[12] Think about the times you eat in restaurants.

Recently, I went to lunch with a group of church leaders in Asheville, North Carolina. As we sat down at a local restaurant, I greeted our waitress Kim, and asked her how she was doing. "Well, I am OK," she replied, but her tone was less-than-enthusiastic. As we prepared to say grace before the meal, I asked Kim if we could pray for her. She gave no specific request, so we asked the Lord to give her an afternoon better than her morning had been.

After our lengthy meal (you know how ministers can shoot the breeze while filling our faces), Kim talked with us. She told us that she and her fiancé were looking for a good church in the area. We told her about a good church, and spent several minutes visiting with her. When we left, she was beaming!

I wish I could say that's the effect believers have on wait staff across the country. I wish I could say that's the effect I've had every time I was served at a restaurant. But that's not the case. In fact, in talking with wait staff, most have a clear opinion about Christians in general. Three complaints typically come up when a server honestly describes why Christians eating out on Sundays are among the least favored customers.

First, we are *rude*. We may have made a joyful noise at church; but let our menu order be wrong and we lose our joyful song. It's one thing to discuss being a servant in Sunday school; it's another to be served undercooked chicken!

Second, we church folks have the most unsupervised kids on earth. They've been cooped up in church for most of the day, and they turn the local cafeteria into play land. It may be cute to us when little Johnny throws his beans across the room; but those who clean up after him miss the humor.

Finally, and worst of all, believers have a reputation as the cheapest

tippers on the planet. It's probably because we've just given so sacrifi-
cially to support the Lord's work. Yeah, right. Maybe some of us are just
plain cheap.

The next time you go out to eat, consider the following: 1) If you're a
cheap tipper or otherwise not an example of how Jesus might treat the
wait staff, please don't pray before your meal. To paraphrase Lincoln,
better if they think you're not a Christian than for you to open your
wallet and remove all doubt. 2) If you're going to leave a gospel tract,
please leave a good tip. A fellow once handed me what appeared to be a
twenty-dollar bill. When I unfolded it, it wasn't money at all but a brief
explanation of the gospel. Clever? No, it was stupid. And believe me,
wait staff won't see it as clever either. I try to leave a twenty percent tip.
If that means eating out less to tip well, so be it. I'm not Miss Manners,
but in the new millennium ten percent is CHEAP.

Perhaps now you're thinking, *I'll never eat out again.* But here are
some simple, positive steps you can take when eating out.

First, *if* you're going to show Christlike love to the wait staff, and tip
well, by all means *do* pray before your meal. You might say to your server,
"We're about to ask God's blessings on our meal. Is there anything for
which we might pray for you?"

Second, make an effort to speak to your server about the Lord. Remember, however, R. A. Torrey's rules about witnessing in public: never
embarrass the person, and obey the Holy Spirit. If the server is busy
doing his or her job, respect that. Still, I have found it takes almost no
time to ask, "Has anyone told you today that God loves you?" Then if
the server responds to you, and if time permits, share as much of the
gospel as you can.

Third, by all means, *do* leave a tract with a good tip. I have seen
people come to Christ this way.

A few years ago, three ministers were eating in a restaurant in southern Indiana. They were on break from a national witness training seminar. As they fellowshipped together, their joy was contagious. They
encouraged the waitress, so she brought them dessert on the house. A
pastor said, "Let me tell you why we're so happy. It is because of what
Jesus did in our lives." Another pastor began to share. She stood there,
listening. As the pastor got to the place of asking her to receive Christ,

she was called to another table. "Another seed sown," they thought. But she soon came back, pulled up a chair, and sat down. Another in the group actually got up and began to pour tea at the other tables. And the waitress gave her life to Jesus. You never know if the next waiter or waitress you meet is a divine appointment from God.

Imagine this scene: next Sunday, across America, thousands and thousands of believers stream from churches into restaurants. In little diners and large cafeterias, smiles are the expression of the day. The patrons are courteous, even if the corn should have been beans or if the tea was sweetened instead of unsweetened. Along the way, thousands of prayers are offered for the servers, thousands of conversations bring up the name of Jesus to waiters and waitresses, most of whom really need an encouraging word. Just how many lives would be positively influenced for the kingdom of God? How many discouraged people, working a second or third job—that single mom, that struggling college student, that weary grandma—could be encouraged about the love of Jesus? Multitudes could be affected—if we not only *say* grace, but demonstrate it as well.

I've seen this happen, in fact, on more than one occasion. Recently, three Southeastern Seminary students accompanied me to Maryland, where I was to speak at the annual Pastors Conference. As we sat to eat in Baltimore, a young lady took our drink order. I asked if she had any prayer requests. She was astounded—apparently she had never been asked that question. She asked us to pray for her studies at college.

After the meal, I offered her a gospel booklet. I began to briefly share the message of the gospel in the tract. She was so interested, she pulled up a chair and sat down. I silently thanked God that it was a slow night at the restaurant. Soon another employee came to our table. I told him he was welcome to listen, and he pulled up a chair as well. In a few minutes both Timmy and Jessica were seeking God for salvation. All because we were courteous, kind, and took the opportunity to share Christ.

Demonstrating godly attitudes when we eat in restaurants is only one example of behavior that will wake up the culture to the message we share. Take a moment and think about other scenarios—when salespeople call on the phone, while at the beauty shop or the doctor's office, on and on the examples come to mind. Just think what would happen if we as one body across the country actually lived what we say we believe. The world couldn't help but take notice.

God is looking for normal, everyday people who can be used in extraordinary ways through ordinary situations. Will you be the one?

chapter four

We're Not in Kansas Anymore

Why the Church Must Change

When you get to heaven you will wish you're in hell
When will you realize, you're already here
You'll thank us now that you've crossed over.[1]

—Marilyn Manson

YOU MAY NOT RECOGNIZE the name Brian Warner. But no person more epitomizes the shift in American popular culture from a Judeo-Christian foundation to a non-Christian, even anti-Christian posture. Marilyn Manson is the name that Warner now uses, and he's the author of the lyrics above. His words exemplify pop culture's dark side, and Manson has become a tragic hero to many disenfranchised and disillusioned youth. In concert, Manson frames his whitened face and black lips with a long mane of jet-black hair. Scars of self-mutilation on his stomach belie his emotionally tormented life.

Manson, or Warner, was born in Canton, Ohio, just over thirty years ago to a father who rarely stayed at home. Early in life, he faced both the shame of being sexually molested by an older boy and the embarrassment of discovering a grandfather obsessed with hard-core pornography. In 1974, Warner began attending a Christian private school. He was not treated well by his classmates and was eventually branded as an outsider. None of these experiences is an excuse for the anti-Christian focus his life has taken. Still, one cannot help but wonder—what if a sensitive teacher at the school, or some classmates serious about their Christian influence, had reached out to Warner. He was around the truth, obviously exposed to it, but the demonstration of Christianity left much to be desired.

As a result, Warner took the names of Marilyn Monroe and serial killer Charles Manson. His 1996 CD, *Antichrist Superstar,* is a clear attack on the Christian faith. The autobiographical album explores the transformation and metamorphosis of a worm, to an angel, to a world-destroying demon. The first song is "Irresponsible Hate Anthem," in which Manson screams, "Let's just kill everyone and let your god sort them out."

The release, which reached number three on the Billboard charts, is a far cry from "Jailhouse Rock" by Elvis Presley. Manson's more recent project, *Mechanical Animals,* and his most recent *Holy Wood (In the Shadow of the Valley of Death)* continue the vitriolic attack on Christianity. *In the Shadow of the Valley of Death* not only draws its title from the Twenty-third Psalm, a *Rolling Stones* reviewer described its "thematic threads weaving connections between Christ and Kennedy, Christianity and violence, [and] mass media and alienation."[2] In fact, at one Web site related to the band, "Church of the Antichrist Superstar," the net surfer is told, "If you want to join the online church and sell your soul to the devil please enter your name." (If you're considering the offer, know that you cannot sell your soul to the Devil, and if you're saved, you can resist the Devil and he will flee!)

Culture has radically changed in my lifetime. Ozzie and Harriet have given way to Beavis and Butthead. Beaver Cleaver has been replaced with Bart Simpson. *The Little Rascals* have been forgotten, swept away in the cesspool *South Park.* The change has come with subtlety, and many feel as though they suddenly awakened in a different world.

What Has Changed?

Baseball umpire Durwood Merrill talks about his rookie year in the big leagues. He called a game in which fastball pitcher Nolan Ryan was on the mound. The second pitch of the game was so fast that Merrill never saw it. He froze, unable to make the call. Finally he yelled, "Strike." The batter looked up at him and said, "Don't feel bad ump, I didn't see it either."[3]

Change is occurring so fast we can't see it. The change has been succinctly described as the shift from modernism to postmodernism. With every generation changes occur, but the changes of the past decades are seismic, comparable to an earthquake that is unparalleled in modern history. Our world has become less decisive, more relativistic, and more individualistic. The change is exemplified by the difference in the tag lines used by Walter Cronkite and Dan Rather on the CBS evening news. At the end of Walter Cronkite's newscast he always said, "And that's the way it is." Far less decisively, Dan Rather says, "Well that's part of our world tonight."

Postmodernism is hard to define because our world changes so rapidly each year. Timothy George and others have referred to this time as an *ecotone,* a time when two or more ecosystems combine. An estuary, where fresh water from a river meets the salt water of the ocean, is an example. The move from modernism to postmodernism is a cultural ecotone.

Modernism

To explain the shift from modernism to postmodernism, it is well to begin with the modern period. Modernism begins with the transition from the Middle Ages to the Renaissance, about the fifteenth and sixteenth centuries A.D. This crossroads ushered in the Enlightenment, bringing scientific, philosophical, political, and theological revolution. We live at the crossroads between modernism and postmodernism, so we see both worlds colliding.

In the *premodern* era, the time before the Renaissance, the view of the world went like this: God knows all, we may know some, but our knowledge is merely a subset of His knowledge. Revelation is key, for human knowledge is anchored in God's knowledge. Such an understanding lends enormous significance to the Word of God, which records the revelation of God to His creation.[4] The *modern* era—founded largely upon

Descartes' rationalism—*cogito ergo sum,* "I think, therefore I am"—shifted focus from the supreme nature of God to man's being the measure of all things. D. A. Carson offers six characteristics of modernist thought:

1. Begins with *"I,"* not God;
2. Assumes *certainty* is desirable and achievable;
3. Is *foundationalist,* you lay a foundation then build on it;
4. Focuses on *methods,* leading to the scientific method;
5. Leads to *naturalism,* which pushed God to the periphery;
6. Leads thought processes to a *historical* truth (i.e., water is water always, no matter what time you are in history).

Modernism had no small influence on the church. Since the Enlightenment, western culture has moved into modernity, and in recent generations modernity, more than Christianity, has shaped people's view of reality. Hunter observed, "The enlightenment taught that human beings are basically rational,"[5] which eventually undermined the place of the spiritual life. "Following Isaac Newton's discovery of gravity," says Hunter, "many western people no longer expected miracles."[6] The need for a revelation from God was minimized, eventually eroding the authority of Scripture. Further, the enlightenment taught that people are basically good, thereby minimizing sin.

The most pernicious tenet of modernism relates to Carson's fifth point above, the rise of naturalism. Hunter observes, "The enlightenment's philosophy of 'natural religion' taught that all religion is essentially the same."[7] This view cracked the door that Darwinism and secularism would, in ensuing centuries, kick open.

Modernism Versus Postmodernism

Modernism is represented by *Star Trek,* the science fiction show that featured a clear objective, "To boldly go where no one had gone before."

> *Postmodernism* has made its mark in the latest
> version, *Star Trek: Voyager.* This later version,
> rather than offering its viewers a clearly
> marked plan, emphasizes, "It all depends
> on your point of view."

Postmodernism

Sweet succinctly describes postmodernism:

> The term *post-modern* . . . is used to denote a 40-year transition from an information age to a bionomic age that will begin no later than 2020. My generation (the boomers) and our children (gen Xers) and net-gens are the transitional generations to this new world. The net-gens (those born after 1981) will be the first ones to really live the majority of their time in the new world. We boomers will make it to the river, but we won't cross over. The crossover to a post-modern world will be made by the generations that follow ours.[8]

"Modernity has not fulfilled most of its promises," Sweet adds, "and so the enlightenment world view has become increasingly vulnerable."[9] For a variety of reasons modernity has failed. Two World Wars, the rise of quantum physics, the absence of any rationally based consensus, and other factors demonstrate the failure of the Enlightenment and thus of modernism.

Postmodernism rejects all of the characteristics of modernism given above by Carson—except number five, the rise of naturalism. Number five, however, causes the greatest problems for biblical Christianity. Characteristics 1, 2, 3, 4, and 6 contain at least the seeds of an objective reality, whereas in postmodernism, subjectivism rules.

In his lecture at Southeastern Seminary, Carson noted several ways postmodernism has affected culture.

1. It feeds the rise of *philosophical pluralism.* In this view, truth is

whatever an individual chooses to believe, a claim that undergirds the practical reality in American culture that tolerance has become the chief virtue, and conviction has become a vice. Philosophical pluralism moves beyond the traditional view that each person has a right to choose his or her belief—even if it is wrong—to state that not only should people be allowed to choose their own views, but that no one has the right to call those views wrong. Accepting all views as correct flies in the face of biblical convictions.

2. It changed the definition of *tolerance*. Formerly, people were tolerant if they allowed those with whom they disagreed to have their say. Now, tolerance means every opinion is okay. The only heresy is in claiming that there is heresy. Television talk shows abound with this belief.

3. It feeds the process of *secularization*. Religious conviction is increasingly marginalized, because it does not matter.

One fact is clear—with the shift from modernism to postmodernism, Christians have lost the home-field advantage in America. A generation ago, even atheists were "Christian atheists"; atheists disbelieved in the Christian God, but the discussion was at least on our turf. Now, in most parts of America, including major universities in the Bible belt, many people have no clear understanding of even basic Christian terminology. During 1995, I was blessed to see God move in a stirring revival among college students and in several churches. God worked in so many places that the producer of the Phil Donahue Show called to ask me to appear on the program. I didn't go, but I was intrigued by his description: "We want to discuss the spiritual 'refreshing' in America." He felt the that term *revival* would not hold meaning or stimulate attraction for viewers. When addressing many in our society, we must begin with the understanding that they know *nothing* about the gospel.

This new world in which we live is called *post*modern, because we have moved *beyond* the modern era. Tom Wolf defines postmodernism as "the exhaustion of modernity, the rejection of the idea that there is an over-arching framework in existence."[10] The beginning of the shift from modernism to postmodernism has its genesis in quantum physics and Einstein's theory of relativity, and its fleshing out in the era of Generation Xers. Postmodernism flourishes in culture today, marked by a denial of absolute truth, and a greater regard for subjective experience over objective reality.

Wolf describes postmodernism as characterized by

1. a rediscovery of the supernatural world;
2. giving equal credence to all alternative authorities;
3. skepticism of the notion of historical progress;
4. a rise of multidimensional authorities—everything from rationalism to shamanism; and
5. a shift from the industrial revolution to the technological revolution.

The changes are so dramatic and so swift that the church, like most cultural institutions, has a hard time keeping up. The shift is further accelerated by the progress from an industrial age to an information age. Long compares the velocity of the current cultural shift to that of a category-five hurricane. His point—many studies compare Generation X to the Boomer generation, but the difference between Boomers and Xers is more than simply a generation gap. Generation shifts have gone on for millenniums. "The more I studied," says Long, "the more I began to feel, and then to think, that I did not have the whole picture. Something was missing. I became more and more convinced that something more than the generational transition from boomers to Xers was affecting this present student generation."[11] He discovered that Generation X was the generation that came of age at the rise of postmodernism. Gen Xers tend to link the church with the failures of modernism. Slaughter observes the result: "The 20–something is absent from nearly all of our churches. This generation is not even finding its way into the rapidly growing megachurches."[12] Gen Xers are the lost generation in the American church.

In 1996, a man was arrested in a ladies restroom in a Wisconsin mall. When asked what he was doing there, the man replied, "I thought it would be a good place to meet women."[13] Look up the word *clueless* in the dictionary and you'll see that man's picture! And the church, too, is clueless in regard to what it takes to reach the postmodern culture. We cannot do 8–track (remember those?) ministry in a DVD world. In

Romans 13, Paul told us to know the times, literally, to be very aware of the season in which we live. We should be well aware of what is happening in our culture.

Certain features of postmodernism relate particularly to reaching the unchurched and are worthy of further investigation.

Pluralism. Postmodernism feeds the innate and sinful tendency of humanity to live apart from God. "Post-modern culture," argues Sweet, "is a sucker for the serpent's lie, 'You will be like God' (Genesis 3:5). . . . Idolatry is very popular today. Celebrity status in America is one example of that."[14]

Any assault on historic and unique Christian thought is actually the reenactment of Genesis 3. "The secret appeal of the serpent's lie," Sweet continues, "is that if we are gods, then we are soul authors of our lives; then we can do anything we want, create any religion we want," Sweet affirms, adding, "Even in church we are prone not to worship someone other than ourselves . . . we go to worship mostly to feel good about ourselves. We want every sermon to be a self-hug. We want every worship experience to pump us up and make us happy."[15]

Slaughter demonstrates how a pluralistic mindset causes not only indifference toward Christianity but actually engenders hostility. "Spirituality is in. Specific claims about spirituality are out. North American culture is not anti-God. It is anti-Christian. Christianity has always been perceived as a dominant threat to the predominant culture because Christianity is presupposed as an intolerant or exclusive perspective."[16]

The recent decrease in the influence of Christianity is seen everywhere. On my computer, my Windows95® "spell check" utility dictionary does not include the books of the Bible. Princeton sociologist Robert Wuthnow talks about one of the dirty little secrets in American higher education, one of which is "its disdain for evangelical Christians. Few groups are as despised as a minority."[17]

Churches are being burned, and now young people are dying in our schools simply because they are Christian. What more must happen to awaken the church? What should we do in response? Cower in fear? Get mad, and then get even? Throw our hands up in abject despair? No, worldly means will not work against worldly forces. Remember, God used an amateur to build an ark—professionals built the Titanic. We must penetrate the culture of darkness with the gospel of light. But critical to doing so is to consistently proclaim that pluralism is wrong. More than ever we must proclaim the truth of Acts 4:12 (KJV): *Neither is there salvation in any other: for there is none other name under heaven given among men, whereby we must be saved.*

Ethnicity. When we lived in Houston, our typical, middle-class subdivision was home to Anglo, Chinese, Hispanic, and African-American families. A few blocks away the street signs in one area were printed in English and Mandarin Chinese. Over 40 percent of new students at New York University in 1996–97 spoke English as their second language, while 50 percent of the Ph.D.s granted in engineering and science in the U.S. went to "foreign nationals," mostly Asians. Some 13 percent of Americans speak another language at home besides English. Sweet expounds on this: "If the 20th century was the American century; then the 21st century will be the Asian century or at least the Pacific century."[18] And Generation X, the first postmodern generation, are not only color blind, they are the first generation in American history to seek friends among people who are different from them.

I speak to many youth groups across America. I often allow a time of questions and answers, encouraging teens to ask any question they have, for truth has no fear. One of the more common questions has to do with interracial dating and marriage. I tell them I find no biblical prohibition to interracial marriage, except in the Old Testament when such marriages were forbidden *because of the idolatry of other peoples.* The stand that is consistent with the biblical message is to date and marry growing, godly believers. That—not race—is what's important. The president of the educational institution at which I teach, Paige Patterson, notes that if Eve is the mother of all people, then we are all kin. The cultural view of interracial marriages has shifted, too: "In 1958, 4 percent of Americans approved of black and white marriages, in 1997, 61 percent. Interracial marriages grew from 150,000 in 1970 to 1,392,000 in 1995."[19]

But the effect of postmodernism has not been to bring all ethnic groups together. On the surface, while the multicultural emphasis of postmodernism seems to liberate all in the name of tolerance, it in fact leads to the destruction of various cultures. Gene Edward Veith notes,

The fact is, real cultures promote strict ethical guidelines. From Mexico to Africa, family ties are strong and sexual promiscuity is strictly forbidden. No culture (other than our own) would teach that there are no absolutes. Contemporary Western culture with its pornography, consumerism, and all-encompassing skepticism toward authority and moral traditions is ravaging traditional cultures.[20]

Rather than lifting up all people by praising their differences, postmodernism leads to fragmentation into ethnic groups, eroding any common ground for discussion. As Veith notes, "People are finding their identities, not so much in themselves, nor in their communities or nation, but in the groups that they belong to."[21]

Only the gospel can truly break down the walls of race or class. Read the book of Acts to see how quickly the gospel collapsed numerous barriers.

Urbanization. In 1870, 10 percent of Americans lived in cities. In the year 2005, 90 percent of the population will be urban. Such a dramatic change has tremendous implications for the church.[22] Baby Boomers will continue to expand cities outward to the suburbs, a phenomenon my generation perfected, moving cities from being centered around Main Street to being characterized as urban sprawl, marked by no centralized area. Gen Xers, however, are in general not following this trend. In more and more cities, the downtown districts, abandoned by Boomers, are being revitalized by Gen X entrepreneurs, as described in a study of the Raleigh-Durham, North Carolina, area:

> The emptied-out brick buildings, storefronts and warehouses are retrofitted into apartment buildings and other multi-family dwellings. Groups of Xer entrepreneurs petition county managers and councils to re-zone the properties so they can be refurbished. . . . Groups of Xers . . . fill in empty lots with stores, turn warehouses into grocery stores and flank the "main drag" with apartment complexes and housing developments that face in toward the downtown district.[23]

Thus, in the future, cities will magnify the shift to postmodernism, especially in the urban communities spawned by Gen Xers and those without either the resources or the desire to leave the cities.

The trend toward urbanization seen among Gen Xers is the outgrowth of another trend. Because of the fragmentation caused by the high divorce rate of Boomers, the rising adult population of Xers and the emerging population of maturing Millennials seek family in a variety of ways. The current, rising generation of adults in a postmodern world find family in the *extended* family rather than the *nuclear* family. For these, "family is who loves you, not necessarily who you are related to. Family is where you find it."[24] It's a sad commentary that for them the show *Friends* more accurately depicts family than does *Cosby*.

The church has a remarkable opportunity to go into these developing communities and help individuals to find "family" in the family of God. Such new communities are, however, being invaded *en masse* by the homosexual community and other groups far removed from biblical Christianity. Will the church seek to honor God by remaining safely in the suburbs, or will she launch into the places where the love of God is so desperately needed?

Pastor Charles Lyons of the Armitage Baptist Church in Chicago presents one of the more remarkable models of ministry in the urban setting. In 1963, Armitage started in a storefront. Lyons came in the 1970s to a church of about twenty-five members. Lyons describes the nation's cities as the cultural mountaintops from which everything flows to society like rain flows down the mountainside. Certain cities, for example, exert influence on specific areas of our culture. Some cities, such as Washington, D.C., affect culture politically. Others, like Nashville, Tennessee, and Los Angeles, California, change society from their position as entertainment centers. Chicago and New York influence culture as major business centers. The bottom line is this—what happens in the cities affects everyone.

Can you think of one bad thing in society that started outside the city? Not likely. Herein lies the problem. Over the past generation, evangelical Christians have fled the cities, or at least fled the inner city to the suburbs. Now, however, the problems of the cities are the problems of the suburbs. Gangs are there, as is drug abuse. Columbine High School resides in suburbia with a state-of-the art complex. Yet a ruthless shooting occurred there. Most school shootings, in fact, occur in the suburbs at the hands of middle-class youth. Why? Because the violence of the city is now the violence of society. Drug abuse, divorce, and alcoholism have reached rural America.

Lyons, who has fought the good fight of the gospel for over twenty years in inner city Chicago, noted that the great cities of America are now more like foreign mission fields—with multiple language groups, multiple cultures, and multiple socioeconomic levels. When I spent time witnessing in the community around Armitage during the summer of 2000, a majority of the people I met could not speak English.

What does urbanization say to the church? Primarily this—because of the influence of cities, we can no longer move in order to avoid the affects of sin. The church must *deal* with these problems in a biblical manner. Lyons observed that in Mississippi, there are more Baptists than people! Why, then, is casino gambling so prevalent there? Because the church has not faced the problems of culture that began in the cities.

The Armitage Baptist Church is one of a multitude that has squarely faced the struggles of the city. A major street gang controlled the corner where their church is located—they are there no more. The liquor store next door lost its license, a sleazy nightclub burned, and a bar went out of business. Why? Because a church stayed and faced the sins of the city.

But if we are to penetrate the unchurched cities, it will take an army of missionary pastors and laity who will battle in the trenches for the souls of men and women. Lyons argues that the process of urbanization is the act of God, who moves people to the place where many can hear the gospel at once.

Reaching Postmoderns

Two shoe salesmen, one a pessimist and the other an optimist, went to a primitive land where the people had no shoes. The pessimist said, "I must come home. Nobody wears shoes here—this is useless!" The optimist reported, "Send me more shoes. No one wears any—what an opportunity!"

Postmodernism is less an obstacle and more an opportunity for Christianity. Great prospects loom for presenting the gospel in a postmodern age. In communicating to postmoderns we can, without denying the timeless truths of Scripture, stress the impact that Christianity has on ordinary lives. We can touch them at the point of the supernatural, on the level of community, or on the failure of man to be autonomous. Many of the failures of modernism are, after all, just that—the failures of an era founded on faulty presuppositions. Christianity existed before modernism; and it will be around after postmodernism. Shall we sit and fret over the challenges before us, or shall we seize the opportunities before us, knowing our great God will lead us?

Long observes, "At the end of the 19th century, the evangelical church had to decide how it would react to theological liberalism. Today, all of the church, not just evangelicalism, has to decide how it will react to Generation X and more importantly, to post-modernism." He adds, "While the consequences to our response to Generation X will last for the next 20 to 30 years, the repercussions of our response to post-modernism could be with us for the next 100 years."[25]

Long is right; and his conclusions ought to awaken the church to the critical time in which we live. We cannot keep doing church in the way we have. Still, a lot of the hype about postmodernism is, in fact, *hype*. True, all the changes described above are happening, but it's too early to conclude that on a personal, spiritual level the changes are as deeply ingrained as some believe. Postmodernism signals the weariness Western culture has with the arrogance of the Enlightenment, with the twentieth century's elevation of scientific reasoning to an almost deified status.

Both modernism with its scientific arrogance, and postmodernism with its relativism, are inferior to the Christian worldview. In order for the church to demonstrate that, we must stay involved in culture while living counter to it.

Timothy George offers some keys concepts to reaching postmoderns:[26]

1. *Be kerygmatic, not apologetic, in witness. Kerygma* refers to the message proclaimed in the early church. Thus, the message of the cross must be our focus over intellectual arguments. Read again the sermons in Acts; note that the content was consistent and clear. We must find new approaches, but we must never stop telling the old story about the cross of Jesus.

2. *The gospel is culture-permeable.* The gospel can be related to various cultures, but we must avoid wedding the gospel to a given culture. Some pulpits, for example, equate self-esteem with the embracing of the gospel. Some make the gospel almost equal to a political party. Such mistakes cause unbelievers to reject the pure gospel out of guilt by association.

3. *Context shapes our proclamation strategy, but not our proclamation content.* Read the sermons of Peter in Acts 2 and Paul in Acts 17. Both proclaim the gospel, but in different ways to very different audiences.

4. *Pass on the faith intact.* In a changing culture clear confessions of faith must be affirmed and maintained, in particular a high view of Scripture. We must stand without compromise upon those doctrines that are nonnegotiable.

5. *Maintain co-inherence of word and image.* Both the truth of Scripture and appropriate Christian symbols, such as baptism and the Lord's Supper, must be maintained in any cultural context.

6. *Promote a critical appropriation of Christian tradition.* Pelikan was right: tradition is the living faith of those now dead, but traditionalism is the dead faith of those now living. It would be a mistake to assume that postmoderns have no appreciation of significant Christian tradition.

7. *Maintain conviction in cooperation with other believers.* In ways that will not violate the conscience of other evangelicals, the church can join together to reach the lost.

Remember that in the midst of rapid changes each generation experiences more commonalities than differences. Every generation is lost without Christ; each age group has the same problem—sin; the gospel remains the power of God for each person; and all people—regardless of how sociologists and prognosticators try to pigeonhole them—need to know God and to know His purpose in this world. Further, the Bible remains the only true written record from God, and the truth of God's Word holds eternal significance for everyone. So let's not so focus on the differences between groups—whether those differences be generational, racial, economic, or geopolitical—that we forget that we are, in essence, all the offspring of Eve, all fallen, all in need of God's grace. And all the unreached need someone to tell them so.

Jimmy Long offers this assessment: "Many see this postmodern generation as a hopeless cause. But I think that the opportunity for revival is greater today than it has been in the last forty years."[27] Instead of, on the one hand, fearing the radical changes going on today or, on the other, uncritically embracing them, we can seize the day through a radical, genuine passion for Christ.

A young woman named Amber represents millions of Gen Xers caught up in a postmodern world. Her family experienced the fragmentation so characteristic of today's twenty- and thirty-somethings; her parents divorced when she was sixteen months old. To this day she has never met her father face to face. While her mother remarried and the family did attend a small country church when Amber was a child, her background is only vaguely related to biblical Christianity. When Amber was eleven, the family moved from Ohio to North Carolina, and at age fourteen Amber turned her back on church. Running with the wrong crowd, she followed a downward spiral that led from one dark path to another.

At fifteen, Amber was pregnant, and her subsequent abortion opened a Pandora's box of guilt. She used alcohol and marijuana to drown her shame, enrolled in an alternative school in Wilmington, and managed to finish high school because she didn't want to fail her mother totally.

After enrolling in community college, Amber continued her substance abuse. This led to further evils, including working as a stripper. She was prescribed Zanex to help her sleep, but nothing seemed to remove the guilt. In the eyes of her peers, Amber was a beautiful, outgoing, successful person, but in her heart she knew that her life was in trouble.

In September 1998, some of Amber's friends were in a boating accident. Two died that night. Amber knew that if she had been the one to die, she'd be in hell. The day after the funeral, Amber decided it was time to go to church. The first one she attended seemed spiritually dry. But she was determined, and continued to seek. Someone invited her to Scotts Hill Baptist Church, where pastor Phil Ortego preached with a passion, and where people seemed to believe what they sang. Amber continued to live in her sinful ways, but felt continuous conviction.

At Christmas Amber went to a church play at Scotts Hill. The drama included a scene of the death of Jesus. For the first time, Amber felt the Lord say, "I did this for you, Amber." She wept at the fathomless grace of God, and that day she met Jesus Christ.

From that glorious Christmas of 1998, Amber began a passionate pursuit of Jesus Christ. She is now preparing for a life of service on the mission field. I share her story because I know Amber, and I've seen the change God has made. With Amber's permission, I share her story because all around us many other Ambers are passed over by the church. Will we let postmodernism be another excuse to remain indifferent, or will we allow stories like Amber's to motivate us, to impel us to reach out with the love and grace of God?

chapter five

Hope Floats
The Coming Youth Generation

P.S. Honestly, I want to live completely for God. It's hard and scary, but totally worth it.[1]

CASSIE BERNALL WROTE THESE words in a note the night before her death at Columbine High School. The next morning at school Cassie handed the note to her friend Amanda.

If Brian Warner, a.k.a. Marilyn Manson, epitomizes the worst of the impending postmodern world, Cassie demonstrates the hope that the current generation of young people offer to America. Cassie's story offers hope for the teeming unchurched youth in our land, because her life depicts a youth marked by darkness before the light of the gospel broke through. Before Jesus Christ radically changed her life, Cassie for a time followed a path not unlike that of Manson.

In *She Said Yes,* Cassie's mom, Misty, recounts how during middle school Cassie shifted from an all-American girl to a dark, troubled, evil child. Even Cassie's youth pastor questioned whether she could be reached, so dark was the path she trod. "In retrospect," Misty recalled, "Cassie's change from a trusting child to a sulking stranger was so gradual that it blindsided us. It was only when we started getting calls from [school] about her ditching classes, when unexpected D's and F's showed up on her report card, and when we caught her in one too many little lies—that we began to take things more seriously. We were losing our daughter."[2] Their discovery of letters filled with hate and darkness led to Cassie's parents taking drastic action. They moved Cassie to another school, isolated her from her unwholesome friends, and forbade her to listen to the unholy music she enjoyed, including the songs of Marilyn Manson.

At a youth retreat, Cassie met the Lord Jesus. Most who knew her were shocked, the change was so sudden and dramatic. Cassie is an example of the power of the gospel and the need to speak the truth clearly to young people.

But, you may say, her zeal for Jesus cost Cassie her life—is that something for which we can rejoice? Yes, indeed it is, for remember that Cassie, the very moment she died, stepped into the very presence of Jesus. Certainly the grief her family and friends share for her is real and understandable. But at this very moment, Cassie carries no sorrow for paying the ultimate price.

And because of her death, Cassie still speaks the message of Jesus' love. Susan Teran, a sixth grader in Wichita, Kansas, demonstrates the power of Cassie's story. She said, "If there was a shooter in my school, I'd volunteer to sacrifice my life. I'd say, 'Don't shoot my friends, shoot me,' because I know where I'll go when I die." How can a twelve-year-old be so bold? "Susan has reached a personal decision," *Time* reported. "One based on the example of her new hero, . . . Cassie Bernall."[3]

The wind of the Spirit blows where it wills, and a refreshing wind is moving among the youth in our country. While seen most dramatically in the martyrs at Columbine and at Wedgwood Baptist Church, its force is felt in thousands of lives across America. Columbine and Wedgewood mark not a rare departure from the ordinary; rather, they stand as critical markers of a youth culture, signifying a new current of influence and commitment.

Those who study generations have observed the shift in this coming group of teens and preteens. In the past few months, not a single week has passed without my hearing of another positive example of the new breed of students in America. The minister of students at a strong church in Florida recently commented, "Student ministers are realizing that this generation of young people [is] not satisfied with the latest game or ice breaker. They want real, honest, biblical substance." Such depth of authentic spirituality is why this generation holds the key to penetrating the unchurched culture.

A survey last week by the Pew Charitable Trust found that the Littleton shooting is one of the most closely followed stories of the decade (Nancy Gibbs, "*Time* Special Report," *Time*, 31 May 1999, 33).

Tom Brokaw wrote *The Greatest Generation* to celebrate the accomplishments of my parents' generation. Beginning with the high school class of 2000, this can be the greatest generation in our nation's history to reach out with the gospel. Perhaps never in American history have youth in the church been more poised to penetrate the culture. In the weeks following Columbine the Internet, e-mail, Christian clubs, and church youth groups witnessed a surge in spiritual fervor. In 1990 the Supreme Court allowed prayer clubs to meet on public school property, if they met outside class hours and without adult leadership. Since then, the number of Bible clubs has exploded in the United States. Most recently, a network of First Priority clubs has spread like grass fire across the nation. I minister in churches all across America, and I'm seeing more students surrender to vocational ministry than at any time previously. God is stirring this generation!

These youth denote a new breed of evangelical Christians. "Unlike their evangelical parents, who often defined themselves as outsiders, today's campus Christians," says Barnard College religion professor Randall Balmer, "are willing to engage the culture on its terms. They understand what's going on and speak the language. Teen evangelicals have their own rock concert circuit, complete with stage diving; their own clothing lines, like Witness Wear; and in the omnipresent WWJD ('What Would Jesus Do?') bracelet, their own bracelet accessory. And now their own martyr."[4]

Why We Must Reach This Generation *Now*

Of the people who have lived on this earth, we are only the second generation to experience a new millennium since our Lord walked through Palestine. Every generation of youth faces challenges, but over the past generation, being a young person in our culture has grown increasingly difficult. Alan Jackson from New Orleans Seminary, at the Culture Shock Youth Leaders conference on September 15, 1998, noted a progression (or I should say, a declension):

- 1950s: youth lost innocence—television became a part of society
- 1960s: youth lost authority figures—institutions were challenged
- 1970s: youth lost love—the Me generation
- 1980s: youth lost hope—AIDS and STDs
- 1990s: youth lost safety—metal detectors, drug sniffing dogs, etc.

And today the extremes are greater and the stakes are higher. We can be encouraged, however, in that—as Charles Finney as well as others involved in past great awakenings has noted—true revival typically occurs after a time of moral and spiritual declension.

In the 1960s, when I was in grade school, the great fear was nuclear destruction. Many families built bomb shelters, and civil defense drills were as common as fire drills. Today, few children fear a nuclear holocaust, yet they still fear, and what they fear is violent crime. Many don't know which way to turn for help. As I watched news reports following the Columbine shootings, I found myself nodding in agreement with an FBI agent: "We once had the family, the church, and the school working together. Now all that is left is the school; and it is not enough."

But not *every* young person wants to join a street gang, die from crack cocaine, have an abortion, or shoot his or her classmates. Something is happening among the emerging youth population, something that stands in stark contrast to Generation X. Could it be the Lord is at work?

A Generation in Context

Those born around 1981—known as Generation Y, or the Net-Gens, Millennials, Echoboomers, or Bridgers (I prefer young people)—represent our present and our future. Understanding how critical are these current teenagers can be facilitated by comparing them to earlier ones in American history. As stated earlier, a new generation stands ready for the touch of God. Certain characteristics generally mark the last several generations. Much research has been done on the Builder, Boomer, Buster, and Bridger generations, as the chart below demonstrates.[5] Many in the media and even in the church assume that the coming generation will continue the moral and spiritual slide seen in the previous generation. I'm convinced that such an assumption will prove to be wrong.

Characteristics of the Generations

Builders	Boomers	Busters (Gen X)	Bridgers (Millennials)
Hard workers	Educated	Disillusioned	Serious
Savers	Media oriented	Abandoned	Visual
Frugal	Independent	Seek high-quality life	Consumers
Patriotic	Cause oriented	Independent	Spiritual
Loyal	Fitness Conscious	Defensive	Confused about family
Private	Rock Music fans	Change is good	Education conscious
Cautious	Activists	Relational	Seek a challenge
Respectful	Interested in quality	Pluralist	Multicultural
Dependable	Question authority	Pragmatic	High tech
Stable			Idealistic
Intolerant			

Richard Ross, a national leader in youth ministry used by God in the True Love Waits campaign, was the first to challenge my old assumptions. He claims that the generation of youth today is a different breed from past generations of youth. Secular writers, too, share Ross's conviction. The significant research of Howe and Strauss provides must reading on this subject. Five distinctives mark this generation of the class of 2000 and younger.

1. They are not pessimists, but are optimists. One survey showed that nine in ten teens describe themselves as happy, confident, or positive.
2. They are not self-absorbed, but are cooperative team members. They grew up on shows like *Barney* and *Power Rangers* that feature cooperation. This may help to explain why team-oriented ministries like Upward Basketball have exploded across the nation.
3. They are not racist, but are colorblind. In a 1999 survey, 82 percent of teens said love is colorblind. If your church is a white-only congregation (which would *really* push the definition of church), do not expect to reach a huge number from this generation.
4. They are not rule breakers, but rule followers. They want to be challenged. Because they want to make an impact, this generation could be the most powerful yet in engaging in personal witnessing. They just need some guidance and permission.
5. They are not distrustful, but accept authority. A *Time* survey of twelve- to fourteen-year-olds in 1999 found that 79 percent looked up to their parents more than to anyone else.[6]

A seriousness, an idealism runs through the current generation of youth—especially among growing numbers of middle school students—that can be greatly used by God. The wind of the Spirit rustles through students.

- Who would have predicted the marvelous response of youth to the "True Love Waits" campaign in recent years, where millions of youth have taken a vow of sexual purity?
- Who suspected that a gathering of teens around a flagpole several years ago would lead to millions joining together annually to "See You at the Pole"? Now, over 2.5 million pray annually for revival in this manner.
- On college campuses across America, God is touching students with a fresh breath of revival marked by brokenness and confession of sin.
- On public high school campuses across the nation, Christian clubs are forming at a rate unprecedented in American history.

Surely God is up to something. But are we ready?

It is a sad irony that this spiritual awakening in young people comes often in stark contrast to so many active, adult, middle-aged church members who seem satisfied to be sanctified. Oh, that God would give us all a fresh fire for Him! But the brightest sign on the spiritual horizon is the growing zeal of multitudes of youth.

Revival Generations

Other generations have seen similar stirrings. It is well known that at certain times in history, God in His grace has poured out His Spirit's power in great revival. Not so well known is that in all these awakenings, God raised up a new breed of young people in the middle of the revival. One of the marks of widespread revival is a large influx of young people into the ministry. The breadth and depth of revivals often affected the youth population more than any other group.

In the 1700s, God stirred Europe—including Great Britain—and the American colonies in a great awakening. God touched the leaders personally while they were young. Jonathan Edwards witnessed God moving in his New England pastorate, in which half the town was converted in 1734–35. Edwards began his passionate pursuit of God as a child, his precocious spiritual zeal becoming obvious in his teen years. George Whitefield, the great evangelist who shook both Britain and America through his anointed preaching, was only in his twenties at the height of the First Great Awakening. John Wesley and his brother Charles affected English society as much as any government official in their day. While John was not converted until his thirties, his radical pursuit for God began in college.

Jonathan Edwards, best known for his sermon "Sinners in the Hands of an Angry God," stressed that awakenings particularly affected the younger generation. Speaking about the effect of the First Great Awakening on youth, he wrote,

> God made it, I suppose, the greatest occasion of awakening to others, of anything that ever came to pass in the town . . . news of it seemed to be almost like a flash of lightning, upon the hearts of young people, all over town, and upon many others.[7]

This revival, which erupted in Edwards's town of Northampton, Massachusetts, spread quickly to neighboring towns and greatly affected all. Edwards would, in fact, write a treatise entitled *Some Thoughts Concerning the Present Revival of Religion in New England*. Edwards remarked further on the role of youth in this revival, while indicting older believers for their indifference:

> The work has been chiefly amongst the young; and comparatively but few others have been made partakers of it. And indeed it has commonly been so, when God has begun any great work for the revival of his church; he has taken the young people, and has cast off the old and stiff-necked generation.[8]

Stern words for our day as well.

The work of God was so great on that generation of young men born just after the start of the eighteenth century that even such notable scholars as Perry Miller, history professor for many years at Harvard University, said the decade from 1740 through 1750 was the most important in the history of our nation; and that was because of the First Great Awakening. By the way, Perry Miller was not an evangelical believer. Even a scholar who claimed no belief in God recognized that one generation could have an impact on a nation for many following generations.

Throughout history since that time, God has stirred certain generations in a remarkable way:

- Young college men in the early 1800s became significant leaders in missions and as pastors. Among them were Samuel Mills, Adoniram Judson, Luther Rice, and Lyman Beecher. The "Haystack Revival," which helped launch the modern missions movement in the United States, began with a group of college students.
- God touched a teenager named Evan Roberts, giving him a burden for revival. Later, in his twenties, God used Roberts as a catalyst in the Welsh Revival of 1904–05, in which over one hundred thousand came to Christ.

More recently, the Jesus Movement of the late 1960s and early 1970s touched a significant number of Baby Boomers, including this writer. Many leaders, in fact, along various denominations and parachurch groups, particularly those focusing on our need for awakening, were products at some level of the Jesus Movement.

To get the story of God's work in young people from the past to students you know, see Alvin L. Reid, *Light the Fire: Raising Up a Generation to Live Radically for Jesus Christ* (Enumclaw, Wash.: Winepress, 2000).

Imagine—if God really is stirring His church in a way not seen in decades, if not generations, we who lead young people must be ready. The Bible and history are filled with examples of youth mightily used of God. Some were only in their teens, some in their early twenties. While only a teen, David gave Goliath a terminal headache. Joseph began his difficult pilgrimage to greatness while only a boy. Samuel while only a lad moved into an intimate relationship with God, which would guide him his entire life. Timothy, who followed Paul as a major leader in the early church, was likely a youth when he began to assume leadership. While a young person Josiah saw the hand of God move during his reign as king. We could add Daniel and others to the list.

Note these marks of revivals concerning youth:

1. In almost every case in history, young people played a prominent role in revival movements.
2. In revival movements, multitudes of young people enter the ministry, or surrender to full-time missions service.
3. In times of revival, evangelism is a priority, often fueled by the zeal of youth.
4. Youth touched by God during these seasons make up some of the most effective leaders of the church in the years following. Wesley Duewal states that a brief period of revival on a college campus can have a life-long impact on those students. When the campus

of Wheaton College was touched by revival in March of 1995, Sharon Beougher, wife of professor Tim Beougher, attended many of the services. After attending one service, which lasted almost all night, Sharon went to the local Y where she met an older friend to swim. As Sharon shared with her friend about how God had moved the previous night, the friend began to weep. "Sharon," this godly woman said, "I was a student at Wheaton when revival came there in the 1950s. I have never been the same since those days." When you have seen the fire of God fall, even briefly, you are never the same.

5. Brokenness for sin and radical obedience, which mark all revivals, are prominent among youth. Students simply have a greater zeal, and a willingness to change, than do adults who are settled into comfortable lifestyles.

What if God began to stir this rising group of young people with an unusual passion for Him? Would we adult leaders be in a position to give godly direction and to lead them with great faith? What if we channeled their zeal toward penetrating the unchurched culture with the gospel?

Mobilizing Millennials to Reach the Unchurched

The best way to reach any specific population of unchurched people is through saved people who are members of that same group. So if we're serious about penetrating this lost, postmodern culture, we will begin raising up a generation of young people who invade their schools and communities as missionaries to the unchurched. An encouraging observation about church life in the last five years is the tremendous zeal that youth show when they are trained, encouraged, and released to share the gospel personally. Several times a year I lead from a dozen to several hundred students to penetrate the culture with the gospel. They are for the most part as terrified about witnessing as any adult; but when they get out and do it, they don't seem to lose the desire to share. Even as I write, I receive e-mails from students at a recent Disciple Now weekend who are sharing Christ like never before. Youth today do not want to hear truth only; they want to experience it. And they want to *share* it.

Studies show a great hunger for spiritual truth among the general youth population. Even an MTV survey found this to be true. When youth were asked, "Do you believe in God?" a whopping 99.4 percent said yes. In a day when the opinion of Christianity among youth has never been lower, their belief in God has never been higher. To penetrate the unchurched youth culture, the church must analyze how it does youth ministry.

First, Refute the Big Lie

The church must alter the way we treat young people. The big lie is that youth are the church of the *next* generation. They are the church *now!* No vibrant, passionate church that I know of has an impact among the unchurched culture without having a strong youth population.

Our culture, both inside and outside the church, encourages teenagers to behave like grade-school children instead of young adults. Soon after the Columbine tragedy, *Time* magazine featured a back page article calling into question the way society as a whole has treated young people in recent generations. Lance Morrow observes,

> Humans, . . . have turned the long stretch from puberty to autonomy into a suspended state of simultaneous overindulgence and neglect. American adolescence tends to be disconnected from the adult world and from the functioning expectation . . . of entering that world and assuming a responsible place there. The word adolescence means, literally, growing up. No growing up occurs if there is nothing to grow up to. Without the adult connection, adolescence becomes a neverland, a Mall of Lost Children.[9]

Morrow noted that, a week before, Leon Botstein, president of Bard College, suggested in a *New York Times* op-ed piece, "The American High School is obsolete and should be abolished." He added, "At 16, young Americans are prepared to be taken seriously. . . . They need to enter a world where they are not in a lunchroom only with their peers."

Morrow then offers a fascinating opinion coming from the mainstream, secular media:

> Maybe we should abolish adolescence altogether. Not the biological part, . . . we are stuck with that. But it would be nice if we could get rid of the cultural mess we have made of the teenage years. Having deprived children of an innocent childhood, the least we should do is rescue them from an adolescence corrupted by every sleazy, violent and commercially lucrative fantasy that untrammeled adult venality, high-horsing on the First Amendment, can conceive.

In 1951, J. D. Salinger published *Catcher in the Rye,* "one of the founding documents of American adolescence." Morrow notes how Salinger describes Holden Caulfield, a young man who was expelled from a prep school. After Caulfield donned a red hat, a kid asked whether it were a deer shooting hat. Squinting as if aiming to shoot, Caulfield replied, "This is a people shooting hat. I shoot people in it." A generation later, life has imitated art.

My colleague David Black has written a fascinating book that calls into question the way the church and society has approached the youth population. Every parent and minister should read it:

David Alan Black, *The Myth of Adolescence* (Yorba Linda, Calif.: Davidson Press, 1998); *www.davidsonpress.com*

Along with many others, I increasingly wonder about the entire approach to youth ministry in the American church. The tendency of building youth ministry on games rather than godliness must be changed. I'm not suggesting we elect fifteen-year-olds to be deacons or install tenth-graders as pastors. But if teenagers can win a gold medal in the Olympics, if God can use a David to kill a Goliath, and if God can use the martyrdom of students like Cassie Bernall and Rachel Scott, He can use a generation of students to influence the culture. Also, if young adults can learn trigonometry in school, they can learn theology at church.

Second, Lay a Foundation and Cast a Vision for Churched Youth

At the beginning of 1999, who would have thought that the last year of the second millennium A.D. would be remembered for martyrdom in the American church? Who could have imagined that these martyrs would not be high profile, mature leaders, but young people? When Cassie Bernall and Rachel Scott died at Columbine for their Christian convictions, and when seven teenagers and seminary students lost their lives at Wedgwood Baptist Church because of their faith, Christians across America took notice. Even the school shootings across the nation in the 1990s failed to prepare us for these tragedies.

This violence that shocked the nation stemmed from the youth population. Perhaps the solution will begin there as well. And God is raising up a fresh generation of teenagers whose focus is on making their lives count. The question is, will the adults who lead such young people in our churches take advantage of this opportunity? Will we continue with business as usual in the church, or will the events in culture cause us to assess the current state of youth ministry in the evangelical church?[10]

In one youth retreat, a group of college students led the weekend, beginning the first service by lip-syncing songs by Britney Spears and the Backstreet Boys. Then a presenter (calling him a preacher would be far too generous) spoke more about the movie *Titanic* than about God's Word. Such an approach is not likely to raise the spiritual bar for young people. But in interacting with those who work with youth, I hear more and more stories about these kinds of presentations. Many youth leaders seem to question whether preaching the Word of God still communicates to students. I respond as previously to such doubts—baloney! An eighteen-year-old recently said to one of my students, "We would rather have nothing than to be offered mediocrity." I think this young man speaks for his entire generation. Our young people long for the meat of the Word, and too often we serve them spiritual Twinkies.

A Fresh Hunger Among Teens

I recently witnessed the hunger in teenagers. God so stirred a youth group at a weekend conference that even public school principals commented on the impact the students had in their schools. I spoke to over two hundred teenagers at the Disciple Now weekend at the Wildwood Baptist Church in Kennesaw, Georgia, near Atlanta. Most interesting was not that God moved, for He has a habit of that. Most interesting was not only what we did that weekend but also what we chose not to do. First, before the weekend, great importance was placed upon prayer. A student of mine and I wrote a twenty-eight-day prayer guide for teens that specifically focuses on seeking personal revival. (You can obtain a copy of this prayer guide at www.alvinreid.com.) The youth pastor, lay leaders, seminary students, and I followed the prayer guide for four weeks prior to the weekend.

Second, the weekend featured no games or organized fun times. I'm not opposed to fun, and I love to play. But many youth ministers spend a lot of time in seeking the latest game for their teens rather than in studying Scripture. We laughed and had a good time; we simply did not focus on play.

Third, an awesome live band led the time of worship through music. They took the kids to the very throne of God. As one of the songs said, God did "light the fire."

Fourth, I presented clear, biblical, and relevant preaching. I'm no great youth speaker, but I preached hard to them. Personal revival, a passion for the gospel, and bold, personal prayer were the themes of my sermons. We offered an invitation each session, and lives were changed. Over twenty-five met the Lord that weekend.

Fifth (and finally), we took the youth out witnessing on Saturday. Instead of going to the go-cart park, we divided up the group of students, let them decide what they would do, and off they went. They did servant evangelism—acts of kindness combined with personal witnessing.[11] One group gave away nine-volt batteries door to door for smoke detectors. The senior girls cleaned toilets at service stations. You can bet some people listened to them.

And most amazingly, many of the youth, when the time came to stop sharing Christ, wanted to keep witnessing. They gave up their free time to continue sharing Christ, and they had a wonderful time. They were on fire!

What did *not* cause the weekend to be blessed was slick marketed materials or the world's greatest youth speaker: I wrote the materials and I did the preaching. No, God moved because of prayer and because we focused on the basics in a format that communicated to the youth.

Laying a Foundation for Effective Youth Ministry

The success of the weekend conference confirms what I've suspected for some time. I speak in a lot of churches, and to many youth groups; and I teach scores of current and future youth pastors. Many youth ministers have underemphasized the basics of prayer, the Word, and witnessing. Consider the following as pillars for building a youth ministry in the new millennium:

1. *Teach students to pray.* Teach by taking them to the Scriptures, by giving specific helps, and most of all by your example. Do the youth whom you lead see you as a person of prayer? We printed the twenty-eight-day prayer guide and presented them to the students at the last small-group time that weekend. When I spoke on prayer, we made a Prayer Wall from a huge sheet of paper for students to sign. Those students had *awesome* meetings the following Wednesday nights, and several school principals recognized the hand of God. Why? Because the students began to pray—daily, fervently, deeply.

> This generation wants not simply to hear truth—they want to experience it in their daily lives.

2. *Teach students the Bible.* Tell them you will teach them things their parents don't know. (In most churches, that won't take much.) It

grieves me when over and over I go to churches and speak to youth groups in conservative, evangelistic churches, and almost no teenagers have their Bible. They don't even need it at church—why should they read it at home?

It grieves me, too, to hear about youth summer camps with no preaching, replacing it with drama. I love drama. But God chose to use the foolishness of preaching, and I have yet to find a way to improve on His will. What young people want and need is clear, honest, straight, *real* preaching.

3. *Take your students out witnessing.* Students today want a challenge, and nothing provides more of an in-your-face challenge than sharing Christ with others. Could it be that youth leaders do not challenge their students to witness because *they* don't witness? Over the past year and a half I've been a part of numerous student groups who went out to witness. Most were scared silly, and almost all returned fired up and ready to do it again. I constantly receive e-mails from teenagers reporting their latest witnessing endeavor. In every case the catalyst for their witness was the time of witnessing as a group. Students today want to be a part of something real, something that matters. The gospel matters!

4. *Teach your students to worship.* Cassie Bernall went to a youth retreat and heard the gospel. The most powerful influence that weekend was the time of *singing*. We dare not minimize preaching; but neither should we underestimate the power of music on this generation. Some people think the way to build a youth ministry is to take them from concert to concert. That produces music junkies, or groupies, not young worshipers. Teach students that worship is fundamentally about giving ourselves to God, not merely receiving a blessing from Him. Teach them the importance of opening their hearts to Him. Teach them to worship God privately as well as corporately. And teach them that great music and wonderful songs open a person's heart so that the Word of God can fill it.

5. *Finally, set the bar high for your youth.* My son Josh had led others to Christ by the age of thirteen. Effective youth ministers tell me that most young people will rise to their leaders' expectations. Why do Mormons' kids, who don't believe the biblical gospel,

give two years of their lives to a mission that *they* pay for, while in churches we fear our youth won't go to a *week* of camp without filling their days with activities devoid of spiritual truth? Because they set the bar high.

Our Incredible Opportunity

In the year 2006 and thereafter, more teenagers will populate the United States than at any time in our history. Further, the history of great awakenings teems with examples of the vital role of young people in such movements. So convinced am I that God is stirring this generation, that I'm focusing my teaching, writing, and speaking ministries much more on students than at any time in my life. I believe God is getting ready to do a mighty work among young people. What if God does this? Will you lead your youth to jump in the river of revival? God help us not to be sitting safely on the shore.

After the weekend at Wildwood Baptist, a principal at a local public school said to the youth pastor, "You can tell a difference in the Wildwood students. They stand up for what they believe in, and their influence has made a change in our campus." Now *that's* what youth ministry should produce. And that is what young people want—not games, but all of God they can get. My prayer for this generation is that of Psalm 24:6—may they seek the face of God.

part two

A Plan to Reach the Radically Unchurched

FEW THINGS DRIVE ME AS berserk as does being told to do something without being shown how.

Part 1 of this book addresses why we should seek to penetrate the unchurched culture. Part 2 addresses how to go about it. Many books cover the subject of part 1. Far fewer move into the practical implementation of strategies or methods. Certain elements are critical to penetrating the world of the unchurched:

- A clear message (A solid biblical foundation must not be abandoned in our efforts.)
- Testimonies and narratives
- Worship that draws unbelievers into an encounter with Almighty God in a community of believers
- Employing creativity at every level to communicate Christ
- Intentionally planting churches whose goal is to reach the unchurched

As you read the following, ask the Lord which of these practical approaches would be worth your investment in order to reach the unchurched.

chapter six

Add Without Subtracting

*Essentials for Reaching the
Radically Unchurched*

MY BUDDY JOHN AVANT is one of the most effective pastors I've ever met. He's also the most phenomenal at sharing Jesus one-on-one. Sometimes his motivation encourages me, and sometimes I want to punch him! He both inspires me and intimidates me in his passion for God.

A couple of years ago, John went to California. While there, he met a lady at a conference, a self-proclaimed atheist with a Ph.D. from the University of California-Berkeley (not exactly a bastion of conservative Christianity). They talked for over two hours. The whole time, John thought at best he would cause her to question her ideology. By the end of their conversation, however, she was on her knees giving her life to Christ. John simply shared the gospel, and would not back down when she questioned his simple faith. John, like the apostle Paul, discovered that the *gospel* is the power of God for salvation.

On another occasion, John boarded an airplane to go to a conference. A stranger tapped his shoulder. "It's *you!*" the man said. Startled, John turned to the gentleman. The stranger introduced himself and told John that he'd been attending John's church. The man, Harry, told John that for years he'd been quite skeptical of the claims of Christianity. Harry nevertheless attended New Hope Baptist Church, and he had just prayed that God, if He were real, would reveal Himself in some way. And there was John on the plane.

John took Harry to lunch and began a relationship with him. Over time, John did his best to answer every question this skeptic had. Finally, after much prayer, John took Harry, who was now his friend, for coffee. John said, "You know, you're like C. S. Lewis. You're skeptical. But Lewis discovered that you have to come to the place where you simply take a step of faith. I've told you everything I know. Would you take that step of faith?"

Harry was silent for at least ten seconds, and then he said *yes*. Immediately he cried out to God on his own for salvation—right there in the restaurant! He and John both began to weep for joy.

No doubt John Avant, with a Ph.D. and years of experience, is more effective than are most folks at sharing Christ with the unchurched. But in both of these cases, John simply shared the gospel. Oh, he answered questions when needed, but essential to both cases was the pure, unadulterated gospel of Jesus Christ. Do you have that much confidence in the message we share?

Bishop John Shelby Spong recently wrote a book entitled *Christianity Must Change or Die*. In the book, Spong argues that the problem with Christianity is its doctrinal convictions. Commenting on the book, Phil Roberts noted, "His thesis, put simply, is that Christianity, as contained in the Bible, is intellectually unacceptable." Roberts counters that claim: "Bishop Spong has missed the point: Christianity cannot change these essential truths—particularly the message of the cross—and still be Christianity!"[1]

I would add that Bishop Spong has the correct title, but the wrong content. Christianity, at least the current form of it in America, *must* change. But the change must be in bringing the church back to her roots rather than abandoning them. Someone told Billy Graham that his simple message would set the church back two hundred years. He replied that he was trying to take the church back two thousand years—back to the Bible!

In the face of a changing culture, the Bible remains unchanged. Some in the church are embarrassed by this fact. The question confronting the church in the new millennium is the same as faced in the first century A.D.—how to present the timeless message in a timely manner. A more pressing question concerns our attempts to reach the unchurched: Do we still believe that the gospel is the power of God for salvation?

Erroneous Attempts to Affect Culture

Several basic types of evangelizers characterize how the church presents the changeless gospel to a changing world. First is the *compassionate coward*. These Christians work hard to understand the plight of the unbeliever. They get to know "seekers," befriend them, and hope eventually to rescue them from their plight. The strength of this approach is love demonstrated to the unsaved. We ought to be sensitive to people who are like sheep without a shepherd, seeking truth. Taken to an extreme, however, this approach loses sight of evangelism in its effort to demonstrate compassion. Any evangelism that occurs involves "stealth" witnessing that's more concerned with making a lost person comfortable than with clearly proclaiming the gospel. These well-intentioned believers seem to fear that unbelievers will reject them. They should be more concerned that unbelievers will reject God.

On the other end of the spectrum is the *courageous crusader*. Courageous crusaders simply tell the truth and let the chips fall where they may. These evangelizers demonstrate spiritual testosterone that's high on courage and doctrinal conviction, but low on compassion and effectiveness. Courageous crusading is epitomized in this attitude, "Those lost people know where the church is, and if they want to hear the truth, they know where to find it." The problem is, their Sunday service is about the last place you'd find an unsaved person. Remember, Jesus came to the world. Further, in the extreme, courageous crusaders have more passion for picket lines and petitions than for communicating the gospel. They confuse the offense of the gospel with being offensive.

The *confused congregant* represents the largest group of believers in America. They have lost a sense of need to reach the world because for them the church exists as a place of fellowship and ministry to members. If a lost soul wanders into the building, fine; but they fail to go out of their way to reach people. They don't get excited about convictions; they just want to be "fed." This group confuses Christianity and culture. They need to take off their bibs, put on an apron, and get busy in the harvest fields.

The final type is the *concerned correctors*. These people want to reach the lost and have impact on culture but believe that the Bible is not sufficient in its historic doctrine. To make the gospel "full" enough, they add new and unfounded interpretations. The current emphasis on generational curses and territorial spirits sounds more like pagan shamanism than like biblical truth. Scripture doesn't teach that Paul rebuked territorial spirits at Corinth or other centers of idolatry. No, Paul preferred to penetrate the culture with the gospel. If he encountered an evil spirit along the way, he dealt with it; but such dealings never became the focus of his ministry. In regard to evangelism, leaders should teach both doctrine and method rather than spend time on such questionable biblical emphases as "spiritual mapping" or on spurious interpretations of the gift of apostleship. The emphasis belongs on a positive, biblical approach that applies biblical doctrine to our culture.

To reach a changing culture, the church needs doctrinal conviction, compassion for people, and the realization that the church belongs to God, not to us.

Evangelizers don't have to choose one approach and neglect the others. God is Trinity, yet He is one. We, too, can balance doctrine, practice, and passion. Still, how to do so is the question.

Adding Without Subtracting: Affirming Doctrine Without Ignoring Culture

The church must make *some* changes in order to reach a changing world. Change in itself is not always bad, and some changes are certainly good. Why use salt to preserve meat when we have refrigerators? Why scream at people when we have sound systems? Why have diseases when we have vaccines?

Some change is, indeed, very good. And although many churches have a genuine desire to reach the unchurched, it is a faulty notion that in order to meet the changing culture, everything must change for culture's sake. A simple approach to change is *add without subtracting*. Start with a foundation of sound doctrine, and then add ways to deal with a given culture. When adding new strategies or a new worship feature, before jettisoning current features determine the foundational, unchangeable, and crucial doctrines of the faith. The admonition in Jude applies today—contend for the faith once delivered. Then add contemporary approaches.

But how do we add without subtracting?

Lay a Sound Doctrinal Foundation

In a recent survey of Southern Baptist churches in the Tampa, Florida, area, 46 percent of the members could not tell someone how to be saved.[2] We are in a doctrinal dumbing-down period unprecedented in American history. It is apparent that more doctrine should be taught, not less.

What is the danger in neglecting doctrine?
That which is *neglected* in one
generation is *rejected* in the next.

Our time is witnessing a decrease in conviction concerning such vital doctrines as repentance and the uniqueness of Christianity in the face of pluralism. By focusing on political correctness when trying to reach the lost world, we may one day wake up to a church in America that no longer believes the world is lost.

Imagine Jesus saying, "Repentance will drive people away. I will only discuss love." Repentance was the first message Jesus preached. We cannot preach grace without likewise emphasizing guilt caused by sin.

Imagine Paul saying, "Maybe I shouldn't talk to those Athenians [Acts 17] about the Resurrection. After all, they have their own gods. And surely I won't dare mention repentance."

Imagine John Wesley in the Great Awakening saying, "I had better leave out any discussion of hell. Someone might be offended." He founded his societies for those who desired to flee the wrath to come.

We must not become so user friendly that we fall into carnality. A preacher told one of my students, "I don't preach on repentance; it makes people nervous." Good grief! An older preacher once told me not to preach about tithing, because it makes people nervous. My reply? It makes *thieves* nervous (see Malachi). Yes, we must speak the truth in love, but above all, we must speak the truth.

One pastor was visited by a couple who asked for God's blessing on them. When he learned that they were living together, he responded, "God will not bless what by its nature dishonors Him." He said that because truth still matters.

Biblical truth lays the foundation on which innovation and contextualization can occur. Christian bookstores are filled with material that encourages all sorts of innovation without a solid doctrinal base. But remember, only when a solid biblical foundation is laid can you feel free to innovate. Imagine playing a game of soccer. Let's say my goal is the size of a doorway, yours the width of the field. "No fair!" you'd cry. Why? Because I changed the rules. We cannot change God's rules.

New is not always good, just as old is not always bad. Some believers are embarrassed about songs that mention the blood of Jesus; others avoid the subject of hell. There's a difference, though, between being contemporary and being trendy. We must distinguish between being contemporary in order to reach a given culture, and simply seeking something new. More important, we must avoid being *chic* to the world rather than being holy to God.

Theological Affirmations

In a compelling research study of believers who came to Christ from a radically unchurched background, my friend Thom Rainer made a fascinating discovery: "The number one draw of the unchurched to the church," Rainer said in an e-mail, "was strong and convictional truth."[3]

In an ocean of pluralism, people are
swimming toward islands of truth.

Is your personal understanding of Christian truths well-grounded, biblical, and coherent? Do you have a sufficient foundation to "contend for the faith once delivered"? To reach out with the gospel, the following areas require sound doctrinal knowledge:

- *Theology:* a biblical understanding of the nature of God
- *Soteriology:* the doctrine of salvation
- *Christology:* the doctrine of Christ
- *Pneumatology:* the Person and working of the Spirit
- *Ecclesiology:* the church
- *Hamartiology:* sin
- *Anthropology:* man
- *Eschatology:* last things

Thom Rainer's myth 6 (p. 25) about the unchurched is that, when witnessing to them, complex biblical truths should be avoided lest the unchurched become confused. But unchurched people have no more patience with a believer's condescending or patronizing attitude than they have with a holier-than-thou attitude. When you share the truth with a lost person, never be afraid to challenge that person to think.[4]

You don't, however, have to be a brilliant theologian. Still, part of the task of becoming an effective witness includes learning the doctrines of the faith. Without such, you'll find it difficult to relate the gospel to culture. By laying a foundation I don't mean simply to develop a good doctrinal statement. You may express the best biblical doctrinal statement on earth, but if you don't put it into practice it's useless. How can we expect the lost world to believe the gospel if they're not sure whether we believe it?

Secular people often, in fact, respond to Christians in three ways:

1. Do Christians really believe this?

2. Do Christians really live this?
3. I believe some Christians believe and live it, but does it really matter?[5]

In the sixties, secular people were turned off by the church because it was too spiritual; now they're turned off because it's not spiritual enough. We need to know the truth that sets us free, and to put that truth into action.

Build a Framework

In Acts 17 Paul presented the gospel to *the* most culture-sensitive, unreached target—the philosophers at Mars Hill. The message was nevertheless direct in its presentation of the timeless gospel. Read this passage, the most important narrative in the Bible for helping one understand how to reach the unchurched. Paul began by speaking about religion in the most general terms. At the conclusion of his message, however, he *began* with repentance, the one truth that many evangelizers tend to avoid. Paul also spoke about judgment. Are we truly seeking to win people to Christ or, by taking care to be inoffensive, are we merely wanting people to come to our church? It doesn't have to come down to a choice.

The world to which Paul preached bore similarities to ours. In the early church, believers were called many things for the sake of the gospel:

- *Traitors.* Because they would not acknowledge the validity of other faiths, Christianity was persecuted for a longer period of time than was any other group. In Paul's day, pluralism was accepted as fact in the culture and promoted by the civil authorities. When the Christians talked about the uniqueness of Jesus and the kingdom of God, their message was considered a threat to the empire. Today, Christians, affirming the uniqueness of Jesus over other religions, can be treated similarly.
- *Intolerant.* The early Christians died for the conviction that Jesus was the only way to God. This grated against the rampant pluralism in the first-century world.
- *Cannibals.* Because of their descriptions of the Lord's Supper as

"eating of Christ's body," some mistakenly charged believers with cannibalism. Today, convictions on issues such as homosexuality can lead to charges of bigotry.

- *Inferior.* Because of the lowly origins of Christianity, including the birth of Jesus in a manger, and its ability to reach particularly the lower classes, many considered Christianity less than honorable. Today, some consider our faith an antiquated system from the past. Paul avoided the temptation to be impressed with the renown, the architecture, and the prestige of Athens. Instead, he became provoked at the rampant idolatry in the city (Acts 17:16).
- *Zealots.* The evangelistic zeal of believers disturbed more than a few. Imagine being a guard chained to Paul! Today, in schoolyards and workrooms, believers are criticized for telling the Good News.

True Christianity runs counter to the culture. The gospel will always be scandalous; it will always be offensive to any person who rejects the call to repent. But making the gospel plain to our culture does not include compromising the gospel to it. As in the first century, one can easily recognize a dedicated Christian.

D. A. Carson demonstrates that Acts 17 provides the paradigm for reaching the unchurched.[6] The following summary of Carson's interpretation could well serve as a basis for developing a local church strategy for reaching unchurched postmoderns. He offers a biblical framework from Acts 17:22–31, noting that this text gives only a summary of a much more extensive speech. Carson identifies nine features of Paul's framework.

1. *Paul established that God is Creator* (v. 24). Beginning with God as Creator rules out pantheism and makes humankind accountable to their Creator.
2. *Paul argued for the sovereignty of God over all the universe* (v. 24). This builds the foundation for the providence of God. "God cannot be domesticated—even by temples."[7]
3. *Paul taught that God is the God "from Himself," or the God of aseity* (v. 25). *Aseity* means God is not only independent of His creation,

but He also does not need it for His own well being. In other words, God does not need us; we, however, desperately need Him.

4. *We are utterly dependent upon God* (v. 25b). Human ingenuity and self-effort are worthless.

5. *All nations descended from one man, so we all face the same dilemma* (v. 26). If the problem is misdiagnosed, the solution will be useless. But as sin entered through one individual (Romans 5), then all are guilty. As a corollary, this truth should abolish any racism, for we are all of one blood. Evolutionary theory actually supports racist ideas more than does biblical truth.

6. *Something went wrong with the universe God made* (v. 27). For the first time, we see a problem. Until now, Paul is building a framework, an argument to describe sin. Something has gone badly wrong in God's creation.

7. *God is not only transcendent—set apart from His creation—but He is also immanent* (v. 27). God is not far away even in our plight. Paul even quotes some of the pagan thinkers to demonstrate this biblical truth (v. 28).

8. *The need for salvation demonstrates the utter failure of idolatry* (v. 29). Paul "cannot rightly introduce Jesus and his role as Savior until he establishes what the problem is; he cannot make the good news clear until he elucidates the bad news from which the good news rescues us."[8] That is, one cannot be saved until one understands one is lost and in need of a Savior.

9. *Paul introduced a philosophy of history.* Many in Paul's day thought history moves in cycles. But "Paul establishes a linear framework: creation at a fixed point; a long period that is past with respect to Paul's present in which God acted in a certain way . . . a now that is pregnant with massive changes; and a future (v. 31) that is the final termination of this world order, a time of final judgment. The massive changes of Paul's dramatic now are bound up with the coming of Jesus and the dawning of the gospel. Paul has set the stage so as to introduce Jesus."[9]

Paul presented a biblical worldview as a means to present Christ. Nothing about the gospel was compromised; yet the context of Paul's hearers required more than a simplistic presentation. He dealt with key doctrines, including the nature of God, anthropology, sin (without ever using the term), salvation, and the future.

How does this apply to evangelism today? We have to find ways to connect with postmoderns without compromising biblical truth. Campus Crusade for Christ, for example, recently produced a booklet called *Life@Large*. It is not a conventional gospel tract that a believer leaves with a person. Rather, it is a guide for discussion that provides a framework in which you can share Christ. Colin Smith notes that in the past, evangelism "was rather like hanging washing on a clothesline that was already in place. You could take texts like John 3:16 . . . and hang them on the line of a Judeo-Christian worldview. The problem in trying to reach postmodern people is that there is no clothesline."[10] Many today can still be reached by more traditional means, but evangelizing on the college campuses of America and, increasingly, in all urban areas requires putting up a clothesline or building a framework. Doing so does not require a group of experts or a huge amount of time. It does require a willingness to engage culture on its terms.

Another simple example of building a framework is found in the *Two Ways to Live* method used by Phillip D. Jensen and Tony Payne in Australia. Their approach includes the drawing of a diagram of six basic points: God is the loving ruler of the world; we all reject His rule; judgment will ultimately come; because of His love, God sent His Son; Jesus died and rose for us; and thus there are two ways to live: our way or God's new way.[11] Jensen and Payne's example has two advantages. First, it is simple, so any believer can learn to share with the unchurched. Second, it is actually not that dissimilar to more traditional presentations.

Later chapters in this book examine in more detail ways to build a framework for presenting the gospel. Chapter seven, for example, discusses an approach to witnessing called the *Net,* which employs testimony and begins in Scripture, not with the Roman Road but with Genesis. At this point it is only necessary to remind you that essentials are needed because our culture has changed so much. More than ever, believers need to know the foundation of their faith, *not* to have evidences to debate their unsaved friends, but to strengthen their own resolve when faced by unbelievers who simply don't think Christianity is relevant to them.

Relate to the Culture

My colleague Andreas Köstenberger, in an editorial about evangelicals and the new millennium, offers a concise yet profound statement: "The Spirit may be conservative on doctrinal issues; it is less clear whether he is equally conservative on gospel distribution systems."[12] To restate, we must be uncompromisingly conservative in our theology and unashamedly progressive in our methodology. Our theology should be black and white, but our lives can be living color.

How do we understand culture? George Hunter offers these suggestions:

1. Culture is the silent language. It speaks without being audible.
2. Culture is the software of the mind.
3. Culture is the medium of God's revelation.
4. Adapting to culture makes Christianity indigenous and incarnational.
5. All churches are "culturally relevant"; some are simply relevant to another culture. The question is, how do we maintain a church culture that honors the Lord and does not sell out to the world, yet does not produce unnecessary barriers to the gospel by confusing church culture with the culture of the past generation?

We must distinguish between pop and traditional cultures. Hunter describes pop culture as social values and settings that are much the same everywhere at a given moment. Popular culture varies little across space, though it changes rapidly and extensively across time. Music popular in Tokyo can be heard in Chicago. Changes are called *fads*.

In contrast, traditional culture varies greatly across space, but very little across time. Changes that occur are called *trends*. In relating worship practices to a changing culture, Hunter finds three categories helpful:

1. Some things should be *abandoned*—hymns that are not understandable; mimeographed bulletins, irrelevant announcements.
2. Some things should be *kept*—such as preaching, singing, prayer, giving.

3. Some things should be *repackaged*—worship style, worship order.[13]

Remember, contextualizing the gospel does not mean compromise. The goal in being contemporary is not that people will like *us,* but that they will hear the *gospel.* Note:

- Contemporary Christian artists should not sing pop music with Christian lyrics simply because it is popular, but because it offers a vehicle to present the gospel to those who would otherwise not listen.
- Churches aimed at reaching the unchurched should not design services that are first and foremost the most trendy and entertaining, but services that clearly demonstrate the character of God to those who attend (and yes, I certainly believe that can be done in a contemporary format).
- Preaching should communicate to this generation, but not at the expense of clearly declaring the Word of God. Many preachers today reject expository preaching, but doing so is an admission that the Bible is *not* sufficient to speak to our day. We do not need to jettison expository preaching—we need to do away with *boring* preaching.

Jim Cymbala of Brooklyn Tabernacle, a church reaching many in the radically unchurched culture, says, "I have found that 90 percent of the time, the problems people describe to me are not the real problems. Therefore the challenge in all preaching . . . is to get to the bottom-line spiritual issue."[14]

But many Christian leaders miss the key spiritual issue. Many well-intentioned efforts to evangelize the unchurched actually become counterproductive: "For instance, it's a pretty safe guess that most teens would prefer Christian rock to classic hymns. The right medium for the right audience will enhance the gospel message; the wrong medium may result in a seeker receiving the wrong impression of the gospel."[15] On the surface this seems a valid observation, but it is actually quite naive. Of course most teens would prefer rock to hymns. And most children would rather play at the church playground than learn a Bible story. And most believers would rather get out of church on time than be delayed, even if the hand of God moved in a service. Many senior citizens would rather take a fall color tour in New England than tell the multitudes of lost people who live there about Jesus. But is this right?

The issue of simple preference, you see, is not so simple. What is the message that we share, and do we believe it? Some Christian rock music is so vacuous that it does more harm than good. If lost youth listen to it but hear no conviction, it simply appeases their desire to live for themselves. Some so-called Christian song lyrics have less biblical content than an aspirin commercial. At the same time, some lyrics tell the message clearly in a contemporary format. Some groups use a pop music sound to reach the unchurched. I've been in services that were quite contemporary and where the hand of God was evident in the lives of hundreds of teens who were ready to assault the gates of hell with the gospel.

Jimmy Long makes the point well in regard to relating to the culture:

> About seventeen years ago, the InterVarsity Christian Fellowship student group had a massive outreach at UNC-Chapel Hill. We brought Billy Graham in for a week and had over thirty thousand people, including fourteen thousand college students, come to hear him. The title of the outreach was *Reason to Live.* If we were going to do the outreach now in the . . . early twenty-first century, we would need to change the title. We would call it *An Offer of Hope.* The speaker would use some of the same passages of Scripture but would offer a message of eternal hope to a people that have no hope.[16]

I recently worshiped in the Armitage Baptist Church in inner city Chicago. This fascinating congregation welcomes many hundreds every Sunday from various races and backgrounds. It presents a beautiful picture of the body of Christ. A great strength of the church lies in her understanding of the difference between preferences and principles. The church is uncompromisingly conservative in her doctrine, and unconditional in her love. That, dear reader, is a combination God can use! Too many today compromise truth in a misguided understanding of compassion.

Armitage features a wonderful mix of timeless and timely elements. On one Sunday, the theme of the singing was the holiness of God. A praise band led the music, and contemporary praise songs were sung, culminating in a rich, passionately sung hymn "Holy, Holy, Holy." In the middle of the singing a responsive reading of Scripture was presented. The pastor preached an expository message. In other words, in the essentials Armitage is solid; in the nonessentials she is fluid.

The tools available today—from Power Point to drama to drums—are neutral in themselves. They can cause clutter that hinders the gospel; or they can enhance the message. But our desire to communicate effectively must always be driven by our desire to communicate truth.

My son Josh loves sports. One of his football heroes—for his faith as much as for his athletic ability—is Reggie White. I got Reggie's autograph for Josh at a convention in Atlanta. The next day, I met a guy on the elevator, a bellman originally from Philadelphia. We started talking about Reggie White, and the bellman said, "He's been criticized for statements he made last year on homosexuality." My reply, before briefly sharing Jesus, was, "Yes, and anyone with convictions will be criticized, because in American culture, tolerance is a virtue, and conviction is a vice."

By the way, Reggie signed Josh's football with Philippians 1:29: "Also suffer for Him." Reggie White's reputation in our society has suffered for his convictions, but he stands for truth. How do we respond to a relativistic culture? We tell people the *truth*. People seek the truth.

I may sound out-of-touch, a professor stuck in the twentieth century who looks with contempt on anything new. But I'm a member of a church with an extremely contemporary approach to corporate worship. It has a full-time minister of drama, some extremely creative ministries, a Saturday night worship experience and three Sunday morning services. And all is founded on a concrete biblical basis. Many today claim that reaching the unchurched is an either/or proposition. Actually it's a both/and ministry. Don't make innovation and conviction either/or; the same can be said for preaching and drama, or hymns and praise songs, or confrontational evangelism and relational witnessing.

What About Apologetics?

Apologetics as a discipline has always played a role in evangelism. But in reaching the unchurched in this new, postmodern world, one must understand the subtle but significant shift in apologetics. Our culture is becoming increasingly like that faced by the early church, which had many apologists who also considered themselves evangelists.

Michael Green describes a scene in the pre-modern, early church era in which a preacher defends the faith in a manner that would be appropriate in our day. A group of skeptics asks the preacher why a small mosquito has six feet and wings; while the elephant, the largest of all animals, is wingless and has only four feet. The question was an attempt to stump the preacher, much as some questions are asked in our day. But listen to the response of Green's preacher:

> The preacher is unabashed. "There is no point in telling you the reason for the different structure of mosquito and elephant; for you are completely ignorant of the God who made both." He could . . . answer the frivolous questions if they asked them sincerely; but he refuses to get sidetracked by bogus issues like these, impelled as he is by the concern to fulfill his commission. The preacher says further, "We have a commission only to tell you the words of him who sent us. Instead of logical proof, we bring before you many witnesses from among yourselves. . . . it is of course open to you either to accept or disbelieve adequate testimony of this sort; but I shall not cease to declare unto you what is for your profit: for to be silent would be loss for me just as to disbelieve would mean ruin for you."[17]

The key ingredient is the preacher's statement about Christians coming from the ranks of the skeptics.

We must reach the unchurched, and when we do, their changed lives demonstrate the power of the gospel. Unchurched Americans are less likely to ask of Christianity, "Can you *prove* it?" They are more likely to ask, "Can you *live* it?" Certainly propositional apologetics will continue to have a role with some groups; for unchurched Americans, however, the greatest apologetic is a changed life.

Long observes, "Most teenagers and 20-somethings rarely ask, 'What do you think?' they ask instead, 'How do you feel?' Thus this is the question that our apologetics need to answer. Some evangelicals are so steeped in the rational apologetic mindset that they consider any alternative to be heretical."[18] Traditional apologetics have a place, for there will always be those who are intellectually resistant. Still, a changed life remains a powerful defense of the gospel.

Today, the greatest apologetic
is a changed life.

Guiding Principles for Reaching the Radically Unchurched

The church needs ministers and laity who intentionally seek the radically unchurched. Certain principles must guide this focus.

1. Begin with the gospel, not the needs of the radically unchurched. Any discussion of evangelism should begin with theology, not anthropology. Developing a process to reach the radically unchurched must never begin with their situation. Rather, we should begin with the heart of God Himself—for who knows better how to reach those without Christ than their Creator? We should always present biblical content and apply it to culture. This is probably the greatest struggle—how to present the unchanging message to changing people.

Paul reminds us that the *gospel* remains the power of God for salvation (Rom. 1:16–17). The application of the gospel may guide our approach; but the truth of the gospel must guide our presentation. In our desire to be relevant, let us first be significant, focusing on the truth of the gospel.

2. Remain intentional in personal evangelism. There is a tendency to avoid intentionally presenting the gospel to those with no knowledge of it. On the one hand, some in the church act as though the radically unchurched are also the totally unreachable. Regardless of this perception—whether it grows out of a lack of compassion for those so distant from the church or for some other reason—the gospel compels believers to intentionally, boldly, and lovingly share the Good News. On the other hand, some believers are so seeker-sensitive that the scandal of the cross becomes lost in an attempt to make the gospel attractive. In a culture filled with spiritual heat but devoid of the light of the truth, the message of the cross must be proclaimed to everyone.

Most who receive Christ do so after hearing the gospel several times. Faith comes by hearing, and hearing by the Word of God. So the more times believers share the gospel with the radically unchurched, the more likely they are to embrace the message. Paul offers the preeminent model of an effective witness to the unchurched; and his intentional approach to presenting Christ is obvious. Whether talking to a proconsul on Cyprus (Acts 13) or to the philosophers at Mars Hill (Acts 17), Paul clearly declared the message of salvation to all who would hear it.

3. *Give specific attention to reaching the younger generation of radically unchurched people.* Thom Rainer notes that 80 percent of those who come to Christ do so before age twenty.[19] Churches serious about reaching the radically unchurched will give great attention to reaching them while they are young. I've spoken in many churches whose priorities send a message: "Give us a youth ministry that keeps our church kids out of trouble, and a children's area that keeps the little ones occupied so we can worship. Then give us a preacher who steps on our toes, but only a little. And let the world go to hell." This critique may seem harsh, but such is the focus of far too many churches.

4. *Focus on divine authority, not human ingenuity.* These precious people have been blinded by the god of this world (2 Cor. 4:4). Reach them, not by a slick five-point strategy to win the unchurched, but by the power of the Living Christ. The radically unchurched in your community will not be won without the expressions of power through a deep commitment to prayer, dependence on the Spirit, and confidence in the gospel.

5. *Raise the bar for Christian living.* The reason many unchurched refuse to hear the gospel is because they have no desire to be like the Christians that they know. Spirituality holds great interest to our culture, but most people do not turn to the Christian faith in their spiritual quest. Today, most unchurched people cannot even define the term *Christian* in the biblical sense. Being a Christian is equated with being an American, or being a churchgoer, or being moral. Many have not re-

jected Jesus; they have rejected a caricature of Jesus that is emulated in the lives of many who claim to follow Him.

The church that will effectively reach the unchurched has members filled with a passion for Christ. The lives of those members demonstrate that Christianity involves more than serving on a church committee—it means a radically changed life through Christ. The key, then, to communicating the gospel to the unchurched is to be *real.* Let the unchurched see the genuine change Christ has made. And the only way to be real is to draw upon the reality in the unchanging truth revealed in God's Word.

chapter seven

Telling Your Story

The Power of a Changed Life

WHEN TALKING TO SOMEONE about Jesus, have you ever been treated rudely? Have you been the subject of profanity or ridicule? Such treatment has not often happened to me, but more than a few people in our society are hostile to Christians. Such is Robert's story. But God can change a man from being hostile toward the faith to being a vibrant witness.[1]

"My life before Christ," says Robert, "abounded with all kinds of things that most people would consider normal—things like taking care of Number One, working hard and longing to achieve success, although I really didn't know what success was. Thinking that life was short, I concentrated on having a good time. Unfortunately, this type of lifestyle left many incomplete sentences and lots of questions. I became so focused on myself that I hurt even those I loved. My misguided perspective on life had significant consequences, such as a trashed marriage, separation from my children, and an attitude that became more and more selfish. Still, my pride would not allow me to admit that something was terribly wrong.

"I was at best indifferent to the church at this time. Sometimes, I was even hostile. It was at this time in my life that tragedy struck, and I was forced to open my eyes. My daughter, who was sixteen at the time, was involved in a serious car accident. Not knowing what the future would bring, I began to realize that there are more important things in life than my wants. I recognized that something was missing; but I didn't have a clue as to what it was. I finally had to admit that I was not in control; but I still did not know who was. This all occurred around the Easter holiday of 1995. Easter was one of the two times a year that I might possibly grace the front doors of a church. As my family and I entered the building, I had no intention of listening to anything I heard. The significant thing that happened was that someone actually went out of his way to ask how I was doing. Of course, my response was 'just fine.' The gentleman did not believe me. The following morning he showed up at my office to ask a business question, or so he said. The truth was, he felt concerned because I looked distressed and wanted to see how I was doing. As I shared with him about my daughter, I became emotional. The last thing I wanted was to let him see me lose control, so I told him to leave. The significant thing was that this was the second time somebody went out of his way out of concern for me—something I didn't understand.

"About two weeks went by and we crossed paths again, this time in a parking lot of a shopping plaza. It was about 7 a.m. and he was 'just there.' He asked if we could talk for just a minute in his truck. He proceeded to tell me that Jesus loved me and that I didn't have to face the world alone. This faithful witness obviously lived out what he believed. Right then, the truth about me revealed itself. I really was a sinner, and not only was I a sinner, but my sin had consequences.

"Again, my friend told me that God loved me just the way I was; and to prove it, He sent Jesus Christ to die for the penalty of my sin. He also said that Jesus didn't stay dead, that after three days He rose from the grave and is alive today. I knew I needed this Jesus in my life; so when my friend asked me if I'd like to invite Him into my heart, I said yes. He said that through faith is how we receive Him, and he led me in a prayer. My whole world has changed since I made a commitment to Jesus. I have purpose in my life with a positive direction. The most important thing in all of this is that my friend didn't give up on me. He continued to be genuinely concerned and took a chance on rejection. This man walked the talk. I will never get over my salvation experience because the love of Jesus was demonstrated as it was declared. Now the sentences are being completed and the questions are being answered. I still have a long way to go; but I know Who is going to get me there. This is the abundant life that Jesus promises to all."

Robert now studies in seminary preparing to spend the rest of his life sharing the gospel with the unchurched. What reached Robert? The testimony of another person whose life demonstrated the message he shared. In this relational, experiential, postmodern culture, the personal testimony of a changed life plays a large role in witnessing.

We live in a culture filled with people frantically pursuing relationships but who experience little personal contact. Radio talk shows dominate the airwaves, while television features increasing numbers of talk shows and interactive game shows. The Internet has opened a new avenue of communication through e-mail and chat rooms, yet the anonymity of the medium hinders true intimacy. We can grab our remotes, speed-dial on our cell phones, pop online for a chat, and touch our palm pilots to check our appointments. But in our user-friendly world, are we learning to cultivate real friendships? Christianity offers the one thing technology cannot—the most personal, intimate relationship available, with almighty God. And through that relationship we can develop true friendships with other people, if we will.

A Narrative Culture

This culture has moved from being propositional in nature to being more narrative in focus. It relies less on statements of truth and more on life stories. Just look at the rise of talk shows, most of which are depraved, but all of which allow people to tell their stories. In the eighties, shows like *Dynasty* and *Dallas* were the rage. Recently entertainment has shifted from soap operas and phony story lines to talk shows with real people. Today, "Reality TV" is hot, with shows like *Survivor* that feature everyday people.

The television industry no longer creates programs like the old *Bonanza* that followed a single story for one entire show. Starting with shows like *M*A*S*H*, virtually every television series features shows with multiple subplots occurring simultaneously, stacked narratives, and many stories. The quasi-Christian show *Seventh Heaven* follows a given theme that is played out in mini-narratives among the lives of various family members. Summarizing the impact of this focus on narrative, Sweet notes, "The problem is that clarity about God is no longer transmitted to postmodernists by impersonal, sequential logic. . . . The step-by-step, point-by-point language of analytic discourse no longer has the power it once did."[2] We see this loss, too, in Christian circles. Characters in programs such as *VeggieTales* bring to life for small children the narrative of Scripture.

We should not be threatened by the increased focus on narrative. Scripture contains, after all, much narrative. And in this culture, the inhabitants of which are so desperately seeking relationships, the church already exists. But one reason the unchurched have rejected the church as institution is the perception that the church is *not* personal. This perception is at times a sad reality. Christianity is a *personal* relationship with God. And what if believers across America intentionally sought out unbelievers in order to touch them personally? In Luke 7:34, Jesus was derisively called a friend of sinners. And people today seek relationships, not an institution. The gospel is personal. Jesus came to earth because of God's great desire to give us an intimate relationship with Him. The reality of the personal, intimate relationship with Christ, and the resulting community of faith formed with other believers will be the means to penetrate the unchurched culture.

One of my all-time heroes is a young lady named Tanya. I first met Tanya when she kept our daughter Hannah in the nursery at our church. Her husband, Ray, was a student in my first semester of teaching. I later taught Tanya as well.

Tanya and Ray were in many ways a typical newly married seminary couple—excited about serving Jesus, so very much in love, and ready to take on the world. Then Ray was diagnosed with cancer. He had a brain tumor. For a period of many months this young couple rode an emotional roller coaster of hopes and fears, joy and sorrow that most couples, let alone newlyweds, never face. The outcome was Ray's early departure from this life to meet the Lord. Tanya was left alone.

Tanya and her brother Sean, who also came to seminary, moved into a low-income apartment complex in the inner city of Raleigh. The two became burdened for their neighbors, most of whom had nothing in common with this pair of Anglo graduate students. Tanya told me the following:

> The people we live and work with aren't involved in a church and seem to have no desire to go. What God has taught me in working with these folks is how He expects us to be out bringing church to them. I sometimes get frustrated with church leaders who still feel that I should be bringing more people to the church building and getting them involved there. What they never see is how Jesus is reaching them where they are and how they are hearing the gospel. I really don't know exactly how we are to reach the radically unchurched, but I have seen Jesus do it and I honestly sit back and am amazed that I get to witness it! I am just some struggling, white seminary student who probably doesn't belong out here. But God has given me a love for these people that only He could do.

Tanya and Sean established an effective ministry in the complex through youth meetings, providing clothes, toys, and other needs, and direct evangelism. They have seen people from kids to drug dealers come to Christ. They decided to put together a tent revival meeting in the complex. The meeting was bathed in prayer and blessed by God, and many of the residents came to Christ because of the meeting. Such an impact would have been impossible had not Tanya and Sean been willing to plant their lives among the people. It's no surprise that the meeting had an impact as well on the believers who volunteered to help: "Although I believe the revival did reach out to an unchurched community, I also watched it reach out like I had never witnessed before to many volunteers who got involved in ministry. Their lives were affected tremendously. Several had never attempted to witness to people before we used the *Net* as training several weeks beforehand (see page 138 for more information). Since then they have become more willing to share their faith and are looking for opportunities to do that."

Sharing the Wonder of Meeting Christ

Christianity means *life*. It means experiencing the presence of God in our daily existence. Too, it creates a unique bond with other believers. I travel across the country every year speaking in dozens of churches. I constantly marvel at how total strangers become close so quickly because of the bond we share in Christ. A Christian's relationship with Christ, and then with other believers, offers immediate comfort and belonging.

But our faith is more than experience. It is founded on truth with a capital T. Our experience cannot be trusted unless it agrees with the Bible. Thus, the Christian faith consists of both precepts and experiences; it is truth unchanged by experience, yet truth that gives us experiences. The message of salvation includes both forensic justification before God *and* a new birth. Remember, the Word became flesh, and we make the story of the gospel live when we incarnate it by our own story. We can tell the story of God's redemption in the context of testimony.

Your salvation, then, is both an objective reality and a personal experience. In the Scriptures we are told that a person comes to Christ through justification. What does that mean? Imagine you are standing before God at judgment (and all of us will). Before the holy presence of God you feel such awe, such unworthiness. And then, a book is brought, reflecting your sin that has separated you from God. It is a thick book, much thicker than you dreamed. As the book is about to be opened, Jesus comes to stand beside you, before the Father. Jesus opens the book, and every page is clean. There is no record of your sin. Every trace has vanished! Why? Because through the blood of Jesus your sins have been erased. You have been justified, made "just as if" you have never sinned. So before God we are not guilty. H. G. Spafford wrote in the great hymn *It Is Well*,

> My sin—O the bliss of this glorious tho't
>   My sin, not the part, but the whole;
> Is nailed to the cross, and I bear it no more,
>   Praise the Lord, praise the Lord, O my soul!

But salvation is more than the objective truth that our guilt has been removed—it is also described as a new birth (John 3). Nothing is more personal or intimate to a parent than the birth of a child. If you are saved, you are God's offspring. He is your Father, who loves like no other Father. He desires intimacy with you.

And this is the message we share. A message of a personal touch— *God's* personal touch. And *this* message can reach the most radically unchurched. The greatest personal explanation of the gospel is a changed life. Many believers may buy into Thom Rainer's myth #4 (p. 25), that the unchurched cannot be reached by direct, personal evangelism. Rainer's survey found, however, that over half the unchurched won to Christ received a personal witness from someone in the church they ultimately joined. Only one-third said that no one had attempted to share Christ with them one-on-one.[3]

The implication of Rainer's findings is that a generation ago evangelism could be successful by propositional truth only. A story of the gospel, such as a testimony, could help but was superfluous. Now, the story of the gospel, as in the testimony, plays a far more vital role. So instead of beginning with proposition and moving to story, at times we should begin with story and move to proposition. Better yet, we should weave the two together.

The Role of the Testimony in Reaching the Unchurched

Frank P. Perdue, chairman of the board of Perdue Farms, said, "Anonymous marketing just doesn't work anymore. Consumers want to know not only what they are buying, but also whom they are buying it from. The people not the logo. Consumer relationship development is as important as product development."[4]

This statement has far-reaching implications for how we reach the unchurched. Just sending out a flier with your church name has little effect compared to a real, flesh and blood testimony of a changed life. "Post-moderns don't want to study under an authority figure," Sweet argues. "They want to study the authority figure. They don't need authorities to help them gain information. But ironically, they need authorities more than ever to mentor them on how to use, perform, and model the information."⁵ Some of my students have printed their personal conversion stories to hand out to people, with the gospel clearly presented, as it would be in a tract.

How, then, does truth and experience apply to reaching the unchurched? This culture has a great interest in truth. It desires relationships. It longs for meaning. And this interest and desire offer the church tremendous opportunity. Your testimony—the story of how Christ changed your life and is making you more godly each day—communicates powerfully in this culture. One vital truth needs emphasis—your story of salvation is about *God* more than about you. In other words, as you tell your story, remember to magnify the Christ of your experience, not your experience with Christ.

Magnify the Christ of your experience,
not your experience with Christ.

Sharing Your Conversion Testimony

As discussed above, the shift to a narrative culture affects our evangelism. "If a Christian offered testimony thirty years ago," Carson maintains, "it was possible to get into strong debate, sometimes even a heated one, over the validity of the truth claims that were being advanced. Part of intelligent Christian witness on a secular campus was, for example, to muster the arguments for the historical resurrection of Jesus, . . . [today] the first question is likely to be, 'Yes, that's fine for you, but what about the Hindus?' . . . [Your testimony] is your depiction of religious experience, decisively shaped by who you are; it is reality for you, but it is not culture-transcending reality."⁶ But in today's culture, individual stories matter more than transcendent reality. And that can be an advantage in witnessing. We tell the story of Christ's life-changing work, not as an end but as a starting point for our witness.

Dieter Zander observes how the narrative nature of postmodern culture has affected Gen Xers: "Busters have never read the Bible, and . . . they don't care what *Time* magazine or some other experts have to say.

But they will listen to your story, especially if it honestly describes the difficult as well as the good aspects of following Christ. They will listen to someone who hasn't necessarily been successful but has been faithful." He adds, "Busters won't argue with a person's story. In fact, it may be their only absolute: everyone's story is worth listening to and learning from."[7]

The sad reality is that most believers have never shared the story of the greatest event in their lives with just one lost person. One reason is the failure of church leaders, pastors, staff, and lay leaders to encourage the saints to share their stories. Another reason believers don't share their testimonies is the failure by many to grow spiritually, so the excitement of knowing Jesus wanes over time. A third reason stems from the misunderstanding of the power of the testimony. Many believers think that if their conversion was not dramatic, it is of no use to the kingdom. Not so! If Jesus has saved you, your redemption is as real as Paul's.

Think about unchurched people you know at work or as neighbors. Have you ever shared with them the story of how Jesus changed your life? A student, a man in his fifties, came to me with tears in his eyes. I had challenged the class to share their testimonies with someone. He talked to his neighbor of many years, a man who claimed to be an atheist. After sharing his testimony, the student was heartbroken when his neighbor asked, "If this is so important to you, why has it taken you all these years to share it?" Not an unfair question.

Perhaps you know people with whom you have failed to share. What do you do? Start by apologizing to them. That's right, ask their forgiveness for being so caught up with the things of this life that you failed to tell them what really matters to you. They will likely be more impressed that you are real with them rather than be offended that you are not perfect. Then, tell your story.

Here are some guidelines to help you share your story:

1. Write out your testimony, seeking the Spirit's guidance. Use this simple outline:
   • My life before Christ
   • How Christ changed my life
   • How my life has changed since meeting Jesus Christ

2. Give adequate but clear details showing how Christ became your Savior and Lord.
3. Use language the nonbeliever can understand (avoid being churchy or preachy).
4. Relive your testimony as you tell it.
5. Relate your testimony to key Scriptures.
6. Be brief (two or thee minutes).
7. After sharing, simply ask, "Has anything like this ever happened to you?" This will open the door to explore the other person's spiritual background and help you move into more of a gospel presentation.

Sharing my story of how Jesus changed my life has a way of moving the conversation beyond religion to the reality of one's need to know God. There is still, even in this post-Christian culture, a respect for God and for those who earnestly seek to honor Him. Stewart Hover illustrates this: "On NBC Saturday Night Live, the Irish pop singer Sinead O'Connor, who was a guest host of the program, ended her last song by holding up a photograph of John Paul II, tearing it in half, and saying 'fight the real enemy.' This sent shock waves through a predominantly young audience that had for several years been consuming images of Madonna's cavorting with the crucifix with little reaction. In contrast, the reaction to O'Connor's act was huge—and telling. The cross as an object of history and tradition, had lost much of its power to shock and convict. The pope, by contrast, was someone known in the here and now and understood via his media presence to be a real human being."[8]

Narrative Evangelism

Narrative evangelism presents the gospel in the context of story. "The church in the post-modern era must continue to tell the 'Old, Old, Story' of the gospel," Long observes. "However," he adds, "the church needs to start telling the story by helping others to consider the plausibility and authenticity of the gospel, not by making a rational defense of its credibility. Narrative evangelism merges 'our story' with 'God's story,' through sharing it with others. Narrative evangelism is preferred in a post-modern context. Since it is more personal, the story invites others to enter in to it."[9] Some have gone too far with narrative evangelism, elevating stories of people above *the* story of the gospel. We can, however, integrate the narrative to illustrate and explain the gospel.

How, though, do we achieve this integration? The *Net* approach teaches believers how to share Christ by merging one's testimony with the gospel.

For information on the Net
approach go to *www.namb.net.*

The Net's approach takes into consideration the changes brought on by postmodernism. It trains the witness to weave his or her testimony into the clear, biblical presentation of the gospel. The following summarizes the Net approach.[10]

- *It is culturally relevant.* Today's culture emphasizes experience, and every Christian has a story. It is their life-changing encounter with Jesus. Those who participate in the Net will learn to share their story in a way that communicates effectively.
- *It is relational.* The Net goes beyond teaching believers another presentation of the gospel. It provides a systematic approach to build relationships with neighbors, coworkers, or casual acquaintances.
- *It is testimony based and gospel driven.* The Net approach is powerful because it teaches believers to clearly articulate their story by combining their salvation experience with the essential truths of the gospel.

The Net approach clearly proclaims Christ, but it simply adds the relational element. The presentation provides the bridge that moves a postmodernist from the narrative of one person to the metanarrative of the gospel. The gospel booklet used in the Net begins by asking the question, "Your story: How will it turn out?" It then takes a person through a process of examining his or her life story, and intersecting it with the gospel message. We need not shift totally from propositional presentations (like the "Romans Road" or "The Four Spiritual Laws") to strictly narrative; there is a danger in relying on a story—even *your* story—over the power of the gospel message. Narrative evangelism must not mean ignoring repentance and faith and the high calling of obedience. It must simply share the meat of the gospel through the packaging of story.

Sharing Your Ongoing Testimony of God's Work in You

Beyond sharing your testimony in a specific witness encounter, your ongoing living testimony is critical in reaching the unchurched. Johnny was living an unsavory life until he met Jesus. His long-time friend, Donald, was an agnostic, totally uninterested in spiritual matters. Donald watched the change in Johnny's life, and after a time he thought, *I'm an agnostic. I'm not sure there is a God, or if you can know Him if He exists. But I don't understand one thing—what happened to my friend?* Donald met Christ and serves Him today.

My colleague David Black employs what he called the CPR approach: cultivate, plant, and reap. You consciously cultivate relationships (go to the same gas station, use same barber, etc.), plant the word of God, then reap.

Every unsaved person, regardless of how unchurched he or she is, can determine three things about you and I as believers. First, unbelievers know if we genuinely care about them. Genuine love for people can trump many differences. People don't care how much you know until they know how much you care. Second, they can sense if we are walking in the presence of God, if the hand of God is on our lives, if we consistently walk with Jesus. Third, they can tell if we believe what we share about Jesus. Many lost people don't believe in Jesus because they aren't convinced that *we* believe in Him.

We must share the gospel in such a way that even if an unbeliever does not embrace the message, he or she will at least become convinced that we believe it.

Small Groups

Another way is available by which your story can invade the lives of the unchurched and make an impact, even if you're very shy and find it difficult to talk to people. Consider small groups, where people get to know one another and, over time, open up their lives. The front porch has been replaced by back yards closed in by privacy fencing. The more we continue to isolate ourselves, the more we will cry in our inherent need for others. We are created to be social, not separate.

Sweet observes a trend that I've noticed, too, in many young, evangelistic churches: "Try before you buy post-moderns will not first find the meaning of faith in Christ and then participate in the life of the church. Rather they will participate first then discern the meaning of faith. The truths about Christ must first be lived before they can be embraced."[11]

Small groups can meet the need for human interaction and provide the unchurched an opportunity to witness Christ at work in a believer's life. At the same time, small groups can meet a practical need. In many areas today, a person is safer walking through the wilderness alone than he or she is walking the city streets at night alone. Small groups help people—through the power of Jesus—to cope with the fear our culture has bred. Contrary to Rainer's myth #7 (p. 25)—that small groups, especially a traditional approach like the Sunday school, fails to reach the unchurched today[12]—Bible studies, Sunday school classes, recovery groups, or some type of support group can encourage people to share their hurts, find help, and provide a safe place to hear the clear message of the gospel.

The very thing Jesus wants the church to do—be out and involved in ministry—is the very thing unchurched people seek. Each individual, at his or her core, needs God. Nothing—not fame, or ambition, or pleasure, or money—can replace God's destiny for an individual. The church needs to help people clarify and simplify, to get to the core of need—to know Jesus and to make Him known.

In 1985, a young lady named Bridgette walked down a street in New

York City when the unbelievable happened. A massive crane atop one of the skyscrapers plunged several stories down and landed on top of her. Amazingly, she was not killed. She was pinned to the street for over six hours while rescue workers and emergency personnel tried to get her out from under that piece of steel.

A construction worker by the name of Paul walked over, sat down, picked up Bridgette's hand, and held it for six hours. Rescuers eventually pulled her out from under the crane and rushed her to the hospital. Bridgette endured one surgery after another. About two months later, when she finally came out of the hospital, the news department at one of the television stations in New York covered her release from the hospital. They asked her, "Would you tell us the one thing that made the difference in your surviving this kind of an ordeal?" She said, "It was that man who sat there and held my hand for those six hours. Had it not been for him, I don't believe I would have made it through that experience."[13]

There is power in the human touch. To borrow a phrase, please reach out and touch someone—for Jesus' sake.

chapter eight

Evangelistic Worship

Encountering the Manifest Presence of God

A FEW YEARS AGO I MET A remarkable group of musicians at a national conference. As they played, they demonstrated a genuine passion for God that transcended their significant ability. I interviewed the drummer, a man named Steve. The Church at Brook Hills in Birmingham, Alabama, of whose praise team he is now a member, was used of God to lead him into a wonderful, obvious relationship with Jesus. His story will touch you.

> As a musician, I happen to have been led strictly and solely to my devotion to God through a church I knew nothing about. I knew nobody that went there. I knew people that went there, but I didn't know that they went there. It was a church that was perfect for me, because I'm a professional musician, and now I am able to serve in that area. I don't know how to fix plumbing, so I can't work on plumbing. I can't drive a nail straight, so I don't contribute that way. But I can play music.
>
> I grew up in Selma, Alabama. We were made to go to a downtown Presbyterian church as a child that was quite dull—ritualistic, rote, joyless, totally devoid of spirit, totally devoid of any

celebration and edification. I stopped going as a child just as soon as I was old enough to win the argument. At about the age of twenty-nine, I lost my first wife in a car accident. I was married again five years later and suffered a gut-wrenching divorce. That same week, the church at Brook Hills was founded. In between and among all those things so much happened—a lot of sin, and disobedient behavior, a lot of things that simply were the result of being apart from God. In the fall of 1996, I entered into a personal relationship with a woman that fell apart rather traumatically. It was about a three-month period of the most absolutely stark, total, painful darkness that I could ever have imagined. I went to therapists, anything for help. I finally decided I would go to church because I had run out of places to go for aid. I somehow knew that was what I needed to do.

I had one friend that plays in the band with me that went to the Church at Brook Hills. I thought he was playing as a gig for money. I had decided to go to ten different places, ten weeks in a row to find some place that would help me heal this hurt. So I went to Brook Hills. The pastor walked out with a big smile on his face. He said, "Folks, I have good news for you."

Over the process of the next several months I attended and asked Jesus to come into my heart. My life began all over and is totally new in all things. It is true. It is real. It is tangible. It's the most concrete thing that there is. Until I met Christ, my entire life seemed as if it were lived in black and white. When I met Christ, it went from black and white to color. On January 11, 1998, I was delivered. It took God picking up a 2 by 4 and clubbing me half to death with the world, but I'm glad He did it. I praise Him and worship Him for it. If you're a person who is wandering, searching, you want to believe it, but you don't, let me tell you, it's true. It's real.

I asked Steve, "What is the one thing about Brook Hills that causes folks like you, who don't have a background of faith, to come to Christ?" His reply: "It's God. It's not what we're doing. It's what God wants. It's a very, very special place where the emphasis is worship and developing a passion for God and the place where people get filled. It's a hospital emergency room. We should have a red cross painted on the roof. It's a place where people go to get healed, saved, and renewed, and reborn. Anything other than that is peripheral at best and unimportant." Many who have been Christians far longer than Steve could give no clearer understanding of the purpose of the church.

When the Unchurched Come to Church

This book focuses upon penetrating the unchurched culture, to reach those who do not come to our churches. It's wrong to suppose that the unchurched never go to church. Many, seeking spiritual help, include church as an option in their quests. Did you know that on Easter Sunday, 1999, even 12 percent of atheists and agnostics went to church?[1] If you reach out, some will come to your church. You want, of course, all of them to come to your church. Part of your likely strategy to reach the unchurched is to invite them to a community of faith to meet Christ. The question is, What will they find when they get there?

I've been in lots of churches, and I'd be embarrassed to invite an unchurched person to some of them. Some churches are unfriendly. A guy named Andy and his wife visited a church, and no one spoke to either of them. The regulars looked at them as odd. It was clear that Andy and his wife were "visitors," for they didn't belong. Even the pastor failed to speak to them after the service. They went to a restaurant afterward. They were greeted at the door by a smiling face. They sat down and were treated like they were special. They were visited again and again to make sure all was well. As they left the restaurant, Andy told his wife he would rather join that restaurant than the church they had just visited!

When a church gathers on Sunday for corporate worship the main focus should be on God. But that doesn't have to exclude the lost. The focus of worship is not evangelizing, but evangelism is a by-product of real worship. Worship should be the wild card that trumps our differences and our prejudices. People whose lives are focused on worshiping God overcome all sorts of barriers. A hillbilly from West Virginia found himself serving the Lord at Armitage Baptist Church in Chicago. He went into the neighborhood, inviting children to church. Betty Cherry is the mother of some of those children. Betty is an African-American woman who spent her life in the city and had nothing in common with a West Virginia hillbilly. But through his influence, this former prostitute, who had lived in drunkenness for eighteen years, came to Armitage New Year's Eve, 1982. She was saved through the witness of a lady named Dawn who, before coming to Jesus, had been a prostitute as well. Now Betty heads the ARMS (Armitage Reaching Many Souls) evangelism ministry.[2]

"Right away I was discipled," she said. "The church became a second home and a second family—at times my first family." Through her ministry at ARMS Betty has reached hundreds with the gospel. One lady was from Puerto Rico—she came to Christ and then moved to Milwaukee where she began an ARMS ministry among the Mong people group. Imagine that—a West Virginia hillbilly touched a black, drunken prostitute who reached a Puerto Rican, who reached Mongs. How? Because truth and love trump our differences. And that is why true worship is so vital. Genuine worship will trump the differences in any congregation.

When someone comes to seek God at a church (and everyone has an innate need to worship Him), they should be able to find Him. In the present day we see a remarkable shift in who attends church and why. In the past, on a given Sunday morning the vast majority of people attending were members of that church, with a few guests. Typically, people were reached through the Sunday school and incorporated into the life of the church. Today, however, especially in newer churches that are aggressively evangelistic, on a given Sunday a large number of people may attend who have never joined. My church currently has far more attending on weekends than the total membership. Unchurched people *are* coming to many churches.

What Is Worship?

Just what is meant by *worship?* Worship occurs on many levels, but for the current purposes the concentration will be on the corporate worship service of a local church. Worship is more than praise, although praise is one element. Worship is more than singing, although singing is one way to worship.

Many today believe that a church service must have music. But you can worship God without music. The primary words used for worship in the Old Testament and the New Testament relate to bowing or humbling ourselves toward the Lord. Worship truly focuses on God Himself. Isaiah 57:15 describes those whom God seeks: the contrite and humble. Notice—those whom God seeks do not have to be theologically trained or musically gifted. They can be former drug addicts, pagans, atheists, homosexuals, or even backslidden Baptists! What they must be is broken before the Lord.

Worship, in the simplest of definitions, means to meet God and leave changed. It is seeing Jesus and magnifying Him in His resurrection; it is acknowledging the greatness of God in the face of our struggles, and as such it is the cure for a multitude of human woes. Worship means we reflect on our life from God's perspective, focusing upon God, not upon ourselves. The sacrificial system of the Old Testament was built upon the foundation of offering some type of sacrifice to God. In the New Testament, Romans 12:1–2 tells us that our acceptable form of worship concerns offering ourselves to God. He is the audience, and our efforts at worship should be intended to bring honor and pleasure and glory to Him.

Worship has a personal dimension. Most of us think of worship as done on Sundays or during other occasions of united, corporate celebration. But worship is also personal, done with one's family or at any other time believers gather to give praise or adoration to God. Worship means more than praise—it includes obedience. That is why true worship goes hand in hand with evangelism. No matter how wonderful your service is on Sunday, if it doesn't lead to a life that is daily focused on the things that matter to God, you have not truly worshiped.

Acts 1 and 2 record that after ten days of worship and prayer, the disciples shared Christ. In the midst of worship at the church in Antioch, God led the believers to send out their best and brightest, Paul and Barnabus, to the mission field (see Acts 13). It is recorded in Acts that even in a time of persecution, the believers gathered to worship God through prayer (Acts 4:23–31). As a result, they were filled with the Spirit and shared the gospel. One of the marks of a truly worshiping church is an external focus on reaching the world.

Worship, then, consists of three elements: substance, style, and spirit. How would you rank each of these in priority? Or have you ever thought about worship in this way?

Substance

Biblical worship focuses upon God, not upon us. If we're not careful, we become the object of worship. We sing about God, but if we only sing about how He blesses us, we have limited God to a divine Santa Claus. Rather, worship is more about giving ourselves to God than receiving from Him.

Notice the difference, for example, between singing "Holy, Holy, Holy, Lord God Almighty" or singing "Holiness is what *I* long for." Both songs offer biblical truth. The danger comes when the focus shifts too much from a God-focus to a personal focus. Examine all the songs your church used in the Sunday services for the past year. Would the message of the songs offer a comprehensive biblical theology? The second most likely place for members to get their theology is from the songs we sing in church.

A service of worship should reflect both the greatness and transcendence of God and the intimacy we can have with Him. The height of worship is not the singing, but the preaching, for in effective worship services the music opens hearts so that the Word of God can fill them. Some churches have lengthened the time of singing and shortened the message time, but we don't need *less* Bible content in a biblically illiterate world. Many effective leaders use the Scriptures throughout the time of singing, thus elevating the focus on the Word. Nor should the invitation be abandoned as some have done in the name of being "sensitive" to the unchurched. Worship is an encounter with God, and meeting God brings changes in a person's life. We should offer to that person a time and a place both to acknowledge that change in the context of the body of Christ, and to give a place for that person to seek out further counsel or prayer.

Certain features of worship do not change, such as some elements in a given service. Having a set liturgy is not necessary, for the New Testament is noticeably silent on giving a specific form. The early church, however, followed a form similar to the synagogue, and the epistles of Paul offer some guidance. The Old Testament provides a wealth of material—from the temple worship to the Psalms—on the concept of worship. Some elements of worship are timeless, but the implementation of such elements—from music to preaching to prayer—can be altered and adapted to different cultures. As stated in chapter six, however, expository preaching most honors God and most clearly presents to listeners their greatest need—to hear a clear, consistent message from God.

Biblical substance need not be sacrificed in a more contemporary worship service. Many churches—and I'm a member of such a church—are more contemporary in musical style, in approach, and in appearance, but still feature expository preaching, evangelism training, and other elements emphasizing substance.

In more traditional churches, the services are often lifeless, not primarily because of style but because secondary considerations plague them. Take, for example, the announcements. In many churches announcements kill the spirit of the service. But worse yet is simply a lack of preparation. God is worthy of our best, and those who lead in worship—whether it is the one giving announcements, leading music, saying a prayer, or preaching the Word—should offer Him their best. Unchurched people who come to our churches will notice if we—by our actions in a service—trivialize the character of God.

Style

Style is often overrated. Some church leaders suppose that if their church implements the right style, it can reach the unchurched. It may reach some, but without substance, the church won't long hold interest. Substance, style, and spirit form a beautiful trinity that can no more be separated than can the holy Trinity. But style is an area in which we must separate preference from principles. I prefer a more blended, even contemporary style. You may prefer a traditional service, or perhaps a very contemporary one.

Although style is overrated, it nonetheless matters.

Few things, in fact, get people stirred up more than a debate about worship style. Should we raise hands? When is clapping appropriate?

The Bible affirms hand raising (although it stipulates raising *holy* hands) and hand clapping, but at all times? Pipe organ or praise band? Robed choir or ensemble? How do we balance spontaneity with form? Some argue that the emotionalism inherent in the singing of choruses leads to a gooey feeling of piety rather than a service of genuine worship. That, indeed, is a danger, and music leaders should remain aware of it. But is a feel-good service any worse than a dead, anemic, intellectual service devoid of any fervor? Both, in fact, are wrong. Someone recently asked me, "Which side of the horse would you fall off of if you had to choose—too much experience or too much dogma?" I said, "When I ride a horse I don't plan to fall off!"

In a worship service, people should feel encouraged to encounter the living God. In the cultural context of the Middle Ages, such encouragement consisted in stained glass windows that depicted biblical stories for an illiterate population. In the twenty-first century, stained glass is lovely, but not integral to the worship experience. Fifty years ago a vast pipe organ may have enhanced worship, whereas a keyboard and drums do the same for Gen Xers. A word of caution, however. We need to avoid amusing people. The term *amusement* comes from a word that means "not" and "muse or ponder." To enjoy simple amusement, no evaluation, no critical thinking is necessary. We should not shy away from seeking a close, genuine experience with God in worship, but we don't have to compete with MTV videos to accomplish this.

Every worship service should, however, be contemporary—meaning to relate the truths of God in a way people can understand. It does *not* mean trying to look like the world. In many churches, for example, pastors no longer wear a three-piece suit and tie. They may go with a sport coat and an open collar, or a tie and no coat, or simply business casual. An informal appearance is fine if the purpose is to relate to the listeners and remove any barriers that a suit or, for that matter, a huge pulpit might create. But if the purpose is to look cool, that's not so fine. I doubt that an earring and a tattoo on every pastor will suddenly revolutionize our ability to reach the grunge crowd. There's a difference between being *contemporary* and being *chic*.

And knowing that difference is especially important for those who lead in worship. I've attended churches that have a praise or drama team,

and on occasion the attire of the young ladies suggested they were singing at a night club rather than leading a service of worship to God.
Contemporary is acceptable as long as contemporary continues to reflect biblical values, which include modesty. For leaders in worship,
whether male or female, the clothing, attitude, and actions (like swaying
to the beat in a provocative way) should not dishonor God. When attending church, one doesn't have to choose between looking like a
Benedictine monk or the latest music video phenomenon.

I was impressed by the Church at Brook Hills (the young, rapidly
growing evangelical megachurch near Birmingham). They led a worship
service at a conference I attended. In the mornings the singers dressed
casually, which was appropriate for the setting. Yet none of the young
ladies dressed in a way that called attention to themselves. Rather, the
focus was on God and on leading people to the throne of grace in worship.

When considering a more contemporary style, a church should evaluate the pros and cons of doing so. Contemporary music is fresh, easy to
sing and learn, so participation is encouraged. The music in chapel services at Southeastern Seminary moves from hymns to a combination of
hymns and choruses. The warmth and the richness in the spirit of the
services are apparent when the latter takes place. On the other hand,
contemporary songs tend to be softer in doctrine, and to stress personal
blessing over the greatness of God. There is movement toward contemporary hymn lyrics with more thoughtful theological content. As stated
earlier, the second most likely place to get theology is our singing. In a
given service, what do the songs say about God? Can people who have
attended your church for some time receive significant understanding of
the nature of the faith? Or do they leave just knowing they "feel good"
when they sing the songs?

Being contemporary is not an issue of maintaining or abandoning
tradition. Songs five years old can become traditions. Some churches
sing recent songs because they like them, while criticizing older believers who long for the old songs. Nor does being contemporary hinge on
singing hymns or not singing hymns; many recent, contemporary
hymns have a depth of theological truth unlike many choruses. Paige
Patterson recently made the profound and accurate observation that
most believers today have not rejected hymns; rather, they have re-

jected hymnals, thus the prevalence of screens and projectors versus the hymnbook.

Spirit

In a worship service, style should not be given highest priority. And even substance can be ineffective if truth is poorly communicated. The most overlooked element of vibrant, even evangelistic, worship is the presence of the Spirit of God. Jesus said that the Father seeks those who worship Him in both Spirit and in truth. Give me a church where people feel conviction about the songs they sing . . . a tear in the eye . . . a fervor in the voice. And I don't care whether the music comes from the eighteenth century or the latest CD. That kind of worship honors Christ.

The early church speaks to the future church in the intensity of their corporate worship. In Acts 4, after facing open harassment by the Jewish leaders, Peter and John returned to the church. As they gathered, they cried out to God in prayer. For them, worship flowed passionately from their experience of persecution. Today worship too often flows from a perfunctory habit formed over years of Sunday religious activity.

In verse 23 of Acts 4, as the believers gathered to pray, they were uncertain about the future. But they did *not* commence prayer by focusing on their circumstances. Rather, they acknowledged the greatness of God. They revered Him as Lord, acknowledged Him as Creator, and praised Him as Redeemer. Then, only after concentrating first on the character of God, did they present their petitions. Even then, their request was not that God make things easier, but that God give them boldness to reach the lost. Now *that* is worship! And at the heart of that worship experience was the presence of the Spirit. Notice the outcome: "Now the multitude of those who believed were of one heart and one soul; neither did anyone say that any of the things he possessed was his own, but they had all things in common. And with great power the apostles gave witness to the resurrection of the Lord Jesus. And great grace was upon them all" (vv. 32–33 NKJV).

In the early church, when believers faced persecution, they focused on meeting God more than having God meet their needs. Only two times in the New Testament did someone ask God to make life easier, and both times God said *no*: Jesus in Gethsemane, "If it could be Your will, take this cup" and Paul in 2 Corinthians 12, when he asked God to remove the thorn in his flesh. The Lord's reply was *no*, but with a concomitant offer of His grace.

That kind of worship propels the church into the world with the gospel. When one examines the mighty movements of God in the past—the Evangelical Awakening in England with the Wesley brothers, George Whitefield, Howell Harris, and others; the First Great Awakening in America with Edwards and Tennent and Frelinghuysen—it is seen that people worshiped God with an intensity and enthusiasm unrivaled by that of other periods. From that kind of worship evangelism springs forth as water from a fountain. The key component in such times is not style, but the presence of the Spirit of God in power. We need today an awakening in America, a God-intervention that calls believers back to authentic, Christ-honoring worship. And a movement of that kind inevitably invades the lives of the unchurched as well.

The rise of Pentecostalism, a denomination that gives much attention to worship and seeking the wonder of God, exemplifies the thirst for the Spirit. While marked by excesses throughout its history, Pentecostalism has risen from its birth at the end of the nineteenth century to 450 million by the beginning of the new millennium.[3]

In worshiping God, it is necessary to give attention to the content of our songs and the content of the entire service. True, style matters to a significant degree, but neither style, music, nor substance matters without the life of the Spirit.

The Power of Corporate Worship— Experiencing the Manifest Presence of God

When we take seriously the Great Commission and penetrate the unchurched culture, one by one, many will come to our services. Not all unchurched people are hostile to the church, and if invited by a trusted friend or associate, some will respond. When they do, we want to provide more than a wonderful experience. We want them to find the Author of our worship.

Read the following story of Judy, an unmarried sales manager from Connecticut.

> The last time I went to church I stood in the back and cried. I thought about the baby I aborted when I was twenty-four. I thought about other choices I'd made and how lonely I was. Everyone there seemed to be with someone and have his or her life together. I do have my professional life together. I make a six-figure income. . . . But I just knew, as I stood in the back of that chapel, that no woman there had ever killed her own baby. I had no right to be in that holy place.[4]

Judy sensed her need of God. Worship, when depicting fully the character of God, can both convict and lead to conversion. This kind of worship, which seeks to exalt God while simultaneously demonstrating the power of the gospel to the lost, has been called worship evangelism.

Sally Morgenthaler describes the characteristics of worship evangelism—and most particularly of a corporate worship service that creates an environment effective for reaching the lost:

- *Nearness*—One senses God's presence.
- *Knowledge*—One leaves a worship service having gained substantive knowledge about God and our relationship to Him.
- *Vulnerability*—Believers are open to God. Lost people are sick of believers who oversimplify the tough questions that are faced by all people, inside and outside the church. Unbelievers seek people who are *real*—and worship, if genuine, includes honesty. Worshipers open themselves before a holy God and make it clear that they are not God but simply seek to worship Him. Perhaps instead of striving to be *seeker* friendly we need to be *sinner* friendly; Jesus was known as a friend of sinners.
- *Interaction*—Worship evangelism means participating in a relationship with God and with others. The unchurched long for community. In this culture we need interactive worship, and an effective speaker can incorporate interaction into his or her delivery. I almost never preach without asking for some physical response from

the listeners—lifting a hand, a verbal response, and so on. Object lessons, the use of video, Power Point, testimonies, dramas, and other means can help to involve believers without compromising the focus of the preaching.[5]

To create an environment with the characteristics described above, one that offers the unchurched a place to meet God in a postmodern era, the church must change.

Hunter offers three options to today's church leaders. First, bond the gospel to cultural forms from the past. Doing so, however, may cause people to reject the gospel, not because of the gospel itself, but because of the cultural forms. Second, impose foreign forms—such as eighteenth-century pipe organ music—upon the church. The third, and best, option is to analyze the culture in order to integrate the faith into the language, music, and style of the culture.[6] Over a hundred years ago, the Sunday night service arose as an evangelistic service. More recently, leaders have seen secular people moving from the Sunday night to the Sunday morning service. Now it is more likely to see an unbeliever at a morning service on Sunday than at an evening service.

The Power of Music to Communicate

Music is a language that can cross generations. Billy Graham, far removed from the youth culture by age, still speaks to huge crowds of teens in his crusades. He confessed that he needed an interpreter to communicate with today's youth, because at times they seem to speak a different language. "Contemporary Christian music sometimes acts like an interpreter for me," Graham said. "Although the message remains the same, our methods often must change in order to communicate that message. New tools of outreach and forms of expression must be used."[7]

Many of the changes in worship services stem from the early 1970s, when the Jesus Movement swept across the nation, touching the lives of countless young people. The movement was not a great awakening, but could be called a revival among the youth culture, and it significantly affected the lives of many, including this writer. Many young adults from completely unchurched backgrounds experienced a radical conversion.

A major factor in reaching these young people was music—youthful music from both the coffeehouses of the day and from the many youth musicals written for the youth choir tours in the 1970s.

Music in a worship service can help to lower the barrier for those individuals who are far from the Lord. Today a movement of praise and worship has captivated the interest of multitudes of college students and teenagers. Contemporary hymns and Scripture choruses can enhance an unbeliever's experience of the manifest presence of God.

Here is a summary of principles for worship and evangelism:

1. *Never worship primarily for the unchurched, but for Almighty God.* Worship should not, for that matter, be done for believers either. But do not worship without thinking of the unchurched. I've attended churches in which I did not know the choruses being sung. No song sheets with words were provided. It's hard to worship when you're clueless about the songs.
2. *Focus on substance over style, but do not forget the power of the Spirit as well.* Style does matter. Contemporary churches do reach more unchurched people. Still, the substance must be given preeminence and the power of the Spirit must be present.
3. *Always seek to be changed, not to be entertained.* When the worshiping people of God are being changed, the unchurched will want to experience it too.

Worship Evangelism Experienced

Worship evangelism is really more of a mindset, a focus of ministry, than a method. It can be conducted in three ways:

1. *Corporate.* The subject of this chapter has been corporate worship in a local church. Just imagine if your church approached each Sunday morning with great anticipation of encountering God and with the desire of seeing people reached who do not have Christ.
2. *Family.* Worship on various levels helps the unbeliever to see the manifest presence of God. The head of a national organization that is focused on evangelism came to Christ out of Judaism in

the early 1970s. He sensed his need for Christ in part because he had a meal with a Christian family. As part of their routine of worship, they prayed before the meal. In that simple time, this man sensed God's presence like never before. One of the ways you can teach worship to your children is to have family worship at home.

3. *Personal.* Your personal evangelism will not likely reach past your personal devotion. Gregory (540–604) said of the Church Father Cyril, "His words are like lightening because his life is like thunder." Perhaps no greater power exists in witnessing than a believer whose primary aim is to know and honor God, for out of that personal worship one learns to think as God thinks, and to want what God wants, which certainly includes the fulfillment of the Great Commission. Further, a lost person can tell if a believer is walking with God. Our culture is dry spiritually, and is eroding for lack of rain from the Spirit of God.

We need a fresh rain.

chapter nine

What's New?

Communicating Truth in Creative Ways

IN MARCH OF 1998 I HAD A wonderful visit to the laundromat. For you, the word *laundromat* might not go with *wonderful*, but read on. I visited the laundromat with a former student named Steve, who was serving as associate pastor to the church where I was preaching that week. Accompanying us were two students, Lori and Jill, along with Jill's dad, Banner. And we brought quarters, *lots* of quarters.

I asked patrons if we could pay for their laundry. One or two said no thanks, but the vast majority could not believe total strangers would want to pay for their wash. "Why?" some would ask. Our reply: "We're simply showing the love of Jesus in a practical way." I walked up to Lori, who was speaking with a fifty-one-year-old lady named Linda. Linda had attended church very little for most of her life. As we shared with her, she was amazed at our small act of kindness. In her case it wasn't so small; she'd apparently brought her family's entire wardrobe! But that was the best ten dollars I've ever spent, because that day Linda joyfully opened her heart to the Lord. Adding simple, intentional acts of kindness to personal evangelism efforts serves as one example of using creativity to communicate with the unchurched.

In Martin Luther's *Table Talk* he writes, "We ought to direct ourselves in preaching according to the condition of the hearers . . . to preach plain and simply is a great art: Christ Himself talks of tilling ground, of mustard-seed, etc. He used all together homely and simple similitude."[1] In a culture that has leaped from the Industrial Age to the Information Age into the Internet Age, creativity rules. Finding new, creative means to communicate the timeless message offers a significant challenge.

As noted in chapter seven, such creativity can never replace the clear exposition of the Bible in a way that people will both hear and understand. Yet, even as Jesus used object lessons, personal examples, and word pictures, we can enhance the *communication* of the gospel (*not* enhance the message) through creativity. True, the possibility exists that seeker-sensitive churches may sell out Jesus in a drive to meet the wants and needs of the unsaved. But we also sell out Jesus as much or more when we never tell anyone about Him, or when we communicate so poorly that no one cares to listen.

Joel Barker tells about Swiss watchmakers. In the early 1960s the Swiss were the premier watchmakers of the world. They enjoyed a nearly 90 percent market share. During the 1960s one of the Swiss watchmakers invented a new style of watch, the quartz model, which was a thousand times more accurate than the old mechanical watches. But the Swiss watchmakers rejected this innovation, saying that they were already creating the best watches possible. Some Japanese watchmakers took the model to Japan with them to develop it. The rest is history; today the Japanese have nearly 90 percent of the market and the Swiss have less than 10 percent.[2] Let us not fear creative innovations that help to communicate the message about Jesus.

Sweet offers an important reminder concerning creativity: "The word creativity is often used much too loosely. By many definitions of the word, Hitler was one of the most creative leaders this world has ever seen. The church must tie the ropes of creativity around its original mooring." He adds, "Biblical creativity is critical creativity. It aims not at novelty, but at innovation that specifically continues the divine work of creation. Not everything new is creative. To be truly creative, one has to be in touch and in tune with the on-going mysterious, miraculous powers of divine creation."[3] Faith Popcorn agrees: "Creativity is not strong enough to stand on its own."[4] Truth must be the foundation of creativity. But the higher the predictability, the lower the communication. Thus, creativity enhances the delivery of truth.

The best commercials on television are beer commercials. Mormons make the best religious commercials. Both offer great presentations, but neither tells the whole story. Go to Las Vegas—does any city on earth have more creative billboards? They're great at getting your attention, but they don't tell the whole story. Creativity in communicating must never overshadow the whole story—the message that we proclaim.

The word *creativity* implies something new and different, and the Bible encourages the new: the psalmists write about a new song, Jeremiah promised a new covenant, and Jesus offers a new life. Our God is the Creator, and we are in His image.

This chapter describes ways to use creativity to penetrate the unchurched culture with the gospel. Such creativity comes on two levels. First, on a personal level, whenever a believer uses his or her unique gifts and abilities to share Christ, that believer demonstrates creativity. Second, creativity can be employed by using aspects of culture, which are not by their nature antithetical to the gospel, to share Christ. Drama, sports, the Internet, and other "secular" tools can be a way to evangelize.

Servant Evangelism: Intentional Acts of Kindness and the Good News

One Labor Day, Pastor Steve Sjogren and others from his church held a free car wash at a well-known sports bar (that's right, a sports bar) in northern Cincinnati. After washing several cars, a stylish import whizzed into the parking lot. The driver popped out of the car, and Sjogren offered to wash it with his group. The man smiled, nodded, and asked whom he should pay for the car wash.

Sjogren explained to the man that this car wash cost nothing, that they were simply showing God's love in a practical way. It took three times for Sjogren to explain this to the man before he got it. He couldn't believe they did it for free! Then, an amazing thing happened. He suddenly began to confess his sins to Sjogren—immorality, failure to go to church, on and on, yet he acknowledged thoughts about God. The man even told about how he'd been a starting pitcher for a major league baseball team until he suffered a career-ending injury.

"This was an amazing turn of events," Sjogren observed. "In just a couple of minutes, I had encountered this man at a very deep level. He had just shared several intimate secrets of his heart with a total stranger."[5] All because a group of strangers did something nice for him.

I've seen this happen many times. So many people, and particularly the radically unchurched, have deep questions and significant hurts, and have no idea where to turn. In a matter of only minutes a simple demonstration of kindness can break down layers of suspicion about Christians, churches, and the gospel. A free car wash is only one example of Servant Evangelism (SE), and it adds a little creativity to your witness.

In order to offer the gospel I regularly take students into laundromats to pay for loads of laundry. Providing free car washes, free sodas in parks, free mowing and yard clean up, or lunch for construction crews are other examples of SE.[6]

For more information on Servant Evangelism
see or order the manual *Servanthood
Evangelism,* by Alvin L. Reid and David
Wheeler, at *www.lifewaystores.com.*

Effective

Servant evangelism gives the believer an opportunity to demonstrate compassion for others. Too, simply being involved in SE gets believers out of the church building and into the real world, which alone can breed compassion for people who do not know Jesus. I used the old saying before, and it's still true: People don't care what you know until they know how much you care. People aren't stupid; they can tell if you care about them. Servant evangelism speaks particularly to Gen Xers on both the giving and receiving end; it builds a bridge to the unchurched and it encourages Xers to share Christ. As Long has observed, "Xers are adapting to a new socially conscious reality with the phrase 'think globally, act locally.'"[7]

To stimulate creativity, Faith Popcorn advocates twisting the ordinary—taking common truths and presenting them in a unique way. She speaks of the "extremism exercise" to find the solution to a problem—that is, go to the very extreme and work your way back to the present. If, for example, people are eating less red meat and you own a fast food chain, you go to the extreme and imagine a totally vegetarian fast food restaurant then work your way back to the solution. This "twisting the familiar" helps encourage innovation without abandoning substance.[8] McDonald's, for instance, took the familiar fried chicken and innovated with Chicken McNuggets; Nabisco took graham crackers and made Teddy Grahams. We can take the timeless, familiar gospel and present it in an innovative way that takes nothing from its essence but refocuses its delivery.

Simple to Do

Servant evangelism requires few resources. Simply put a rubber band around a pack of light bulbs and a gospel tract, for instance, and maybe a flyer about your church, and hit the streets. Or if you're resourceful, you might give out golf balls with your church name stamped on them, and say, "This will be the best drive you ever make." My son and I have gone door-to-door giving away information on our church with microwave popcorn. When we say, "Just pop on in to see us," people chuckle, but you'd be amazed how such a simple act of kindness opens conversations to share the gospel.

Relates the Gospel in a Clear Manner

People in a postmodern culture need a demonstration of the gospel to go with the explanation of the gospel. Acts of kindness often cause people to ask, "Why are you doing this?" How many times, after all, has someone washed your car for free, or carried your groceries to the car, or cleaned the toilets at your business? When asked, simply reply, "We are showing the love of Jesus in a practical way." No one has ever refused to take a tract from me, and many, many times I've been able to share Christ.

A Variety of Approaches Encourages Creativity

I've mentioned only a few examples of SE. I was recently at the First Baptist Church of Charlotte, North Carolina, for an evangelism day. After hearing me teach on this concept in the morning, a couple of hundred people spent the afternoon giving away snow cones at the park, giving cookies to local fire stations, going door to door and offering nine-volt batteries for smoke detectors, and showing the love of Jesus in many other ways. Several people came to Christ, at least one very successful Bible study was started in an unchurched apartment complex, and many believers became suddenly very energized to share Christ. Of all the methods I recommend, SE is the best way to get folks out of the sanctuary and into the real world, to share Christ where the unchurched live.

Encourages Believers by Making Evangelism Fun

Servant evangelism is for cowards; the most timid people seem to enjoy it. Just remember to keep evangelism at the forefront. Servant Evangelism is more invitational than confrontational. Why not get a few folks together at your church and do a free car wash in a high traffic area and see what happens? You may be surprised!

Drama

My church utilizes contemporary and innovative approaches without surrendering such timeless elements as the preaching of the cross, the public invitation, door-to-door evangelism, and standard witness training (Evangelism Explosion). Yet we also feature a kicking praise band and one of the finest drama ministries in the country. In fact, we have a full-time minister of drama who has a Master of Divinity degree (he even took my evangelism class!). We are reaching the unchurched without surrendering our allegiance to God. Every year literally thousands come to presentations at Halloween and Easter. We have to take reservations, and at times we have been forced to turn people away. Drama can be one of the most powerful media today to reach people. In many churches drama is the most effective way to get young people plugged into the life of the church. Our Easter presentation for 2001 was called "Jesus the Rock: Alive in Concert!" It began with the resurrection and flowed through history, offering vignettes on great saints such as Patrick, Martin Luther, Susannah Wesley, Jim Elliott, C. S. Lewis, and Franklin Graham. I was moved to tears more than once by the incredible portrayal of such godly men and women.

While I strongly advocate the use of drama, I do suggest that there are inherent dangers to avoid:

Drama can take one's focus off the Word. Christianity is based on proclamation. It is God's choice to use the foolishness of preaching. So the arts may enhance communication of the message, but must never totally replace it. If, for example, preaching is mediocre, and the arts are great, people infer that the Word is less important than experience.

Once I attended a conference on innovative churches. All the best-known names were there—Rick Warren, Bill Hybels, Leith Anderson, and Tom Wolf, among others. One of the breakout conferences was led by two pastors and a drama professor from an evangelical school. The drama teacher became enthused during his presentation, saying that he looked forward to the day when sermons could be replaced on a weekly basis by dramatic presentations. I almost came unglued. I was relieved that the two pastors graciously, but clearly and firmly, reminded the teacher and the class that preaching, the clear proclamation of the Word of God, is a timeless, biblical, and essential part of the Christian church.

What, then, is the place of creative arts? Should we avoid them completely? Are they too worldly for any value to the Lord? Certainly not. I believe arts, such as drama, can have the same effect as music in a worship service. An effective drama cannot take the place of biblically faithful preaching of God's Word, but it can do one of several things. First, it can prepare the congregation to hear the Word. Second, it can illustrate or apply some aspect of the message. Third, at times it can replace the message, as in a special Easter presentation like that noted above.

Creative arts have far more uses, however, than in the Sunday service or for special presentations. Dramatic presentations in the public arena can be a creative way to take the gospel to the masses outside the church walls.

Those in the dramatic arts are tempted to preserve the artistic form of drama and forget that it is a tool. Those gifted in the arts, just as those gifted in music, must take care not to become enamored with the art form over passion for God. Drama is a medium to share the message. When you order a milkshake at the local fast food restaurant, you don't care much about the straw. You may prefer one shake flavor to the other, but you don't choose a restaurant based on the design of its straws. The straw is drama—the shake is the gospel.

The dramatic arts can consume enormous amounts of the body's energy. Drama takes enormous energy and can become counterproductive. One must take care, then, that a church's dramatic ministry not exhaust it of teachers and other leaders. This caution applies to any ministry. Some churches with private schools, for instance, become excessively consumed with the school; some churches in resort areas can be so focused on the tourists that they forget the locals.

By nature drama tends toward entertainment over instruction. Entertainment seeks first to please the people, whereas the primary aim of drama in the life of a church should always be to honor God. The danger of removing the offense of the cross in the name of drama is a real one. That being said, the appropriate use of humor, either in preaching or drama, communicates vital truth in a memorable manner. There is nothing wrong with appropriate humor, and Sweet recalled one of C. S. Lewis's greatest insights: the Devil has no sense of humor. One of the great signs of evil is, in fact, the absence of humor.[9]

With the above cautions in mind, Sweet notes that the "Post-modern Renaissance will be led by artists who love God." He asks, "Is your church celebrating the Artisan in its midst?"[10]

Byron Spradlin is president of Artists in Christian Testimony, an organization committed to sharing Christ through the arts. Spradlin is a leader in a vanguard of evangelicals whose primary aim is to present the gospel through the arts. Consider his thoughts on the subject:

> The jewel of human activity, the activity of worship—worship that must make sense to us in the context of our culture if it is to have meaning at all—demands more than just "propositions of fact." Worship that moves us toward the edges of our human capacities to express requires symbols and metaphors and ritu-

als that help us connect with the invisible realities of God Himself. That kind of worship—private or public—demands we take the realities of God and His truths beyond the languages of the head into the languages of the heart. And that realm, for lack of any better terms, is the realm of artistic expression.

Also, if God intends that artistic expression—or better stated, imaginative and creative human expressions—be used to more fully and more humanly declare His reality, and to proclaim to humans who've lost their way to Him that they access Him and find salvation, then it stands to reason that those believers God has designed with unusual capacity for imaginative and beautiful creative expression play a very important role in leading His people into worship and proclamation.

In fact, the believing community will be out of God's will if it does not aggressively and intentionally move to encourage and include artistic Kingdom-servants. Without them, the Church is not relying upon those whom God designed especially for the role of creative and beautiful declaration of His glory and the proclamation of His salvation. . . . God is already doing [much] in deploying arts ministry specialists for His mission of world evangelization. But . . . again I ask: What does all this mean for Christians and the Church today? Answer: Read the signs of the times! God is doing something special—again! He's moving in new types of people, in order to reach new kinds of people, cultures, and sub-cultures. Pause for a moment. Look around and pray. Take note of who God is raising up—along side you and others—and who are being drawn into God's world mission. Who is it? Arts ministry specialists, that's who![11]

I wish I had more space to encourage the painters and sculptors and others to use their abilities in the harvest fields. It is grievous that the best-known artists are more likely to find acceptance among gays than among evangelicals. Maybe we can change this trend to the glory of God. Noting the cautions above, we have an opportunity to allow gifted believers to flourish and to share Christ in an unprecedented way with the unchurched.

Mass Media

At its best, Christianity has been at the front edge of technology. The printing press did not compromise God's Word; it gave the Bible to the masses. Media can work, too, for evangelicalism. Says Sweet, "Electronic media is to the 'Reformation' of the 21st century what Gutenberg's press was to the Reformation of the 16th and 17th century."[12]

Yet much of today's media-produced endeavors at "spirituality" have little to do with the gospel. True, spirituality is hot on television and in the movies. You can be *Touched by an Angel* and end up in *Seventh Heaven*. But many shows range from the innocuous to the profane, and occult themes abound.

Yet the media reflects two phenomena that are of interest to the church. First, a great interest in spirituality is at work in the culture. Second, that interest is courted by a variety of competing faith messages. Besides the gospel of pop culture, interest is evident in paganism, witchcraft, and gothic themes. The distant past is also of great interest to this generation. They are looking for hooks to hang onto in the midst of a changing culture.

For instance, the first major movie produced by Dreamworks—the company formed by Steven Spielberg, Jeffery Katzenberg, and David Geffen, the latest triumvirate of movie moguls—was the *Prince of Egypt*. Movies and shows that relate to Eastern spirituality are popular as well. Even the rich and famous are taking more interest in spiritual subjects.

The trend spills over into music as well, with spiritual themes finding their way across the musical genres from R & B to C & W. Bob Carlisle's sentimental "Butterfly Kisses" was released as a Christian song and reached the top of the secular adult contemporary charts. Jars of Clay and Kirk Franklin were named top billboard 200 album artists in 1996. The first gospel music video ever to appear on MTV was Franklin's video "Stomp." Wolf states, "Until we sing our way into evangelism we probably will not regain it in the modern church."[13]

As will be discussed in more detail below, God is also popular on the Internet. By early 1997, 15 percent of the Web sites on the Net were Christian Web sites. In 1997, Christianity Online was named one of the most popular sites on America Online.[14]

It seems, then, that the postmodern reformation seeks not to make a brand new church in the sense of jettisoning the old culture. It seeks a church that builds upon the old traditions and reworks them for the new day. That spiritual themes are popping up in pop culture doesn't mean, however, that people are about to trample down the doors of every local church. People are not seeking necessarily religion, particularly the organized kind. They *are* seeking to know God personally. And the church can use mass media as another way to introduce people to Jesus. The church where I am a member is putting commercials on the air, but *not* on Christian networks. We are advertising on CNN, ESPN, and MTV. That's where to reach the unchurched.

How pervasive is television? More Americans own a television set—about 99.9 percent—than have indoor plumbing—97 percent. *See,* not *read,* is the word for this generation. By age five a child watches more than five thousand hours of television. By age seven that same child will have watched twenty thousand commercials a year. The church has missed a golden opportunity with television over the past few decades. Our culture is different today, in no small part because of the birth about 1980 of MTV, CNN, and ESPN. Relative to Christianity, 1980s television sparks images of hypocrisy and corruption. Even as Bakker and Swaggert were falling, MTV was rising and is now a powerful force in culture, not only in its music, but also in politics and social views. (Its views are almost exclusively leftist.) In a typical week, 38 percent of Xers watch MTV.[15]

Much of today's Christian television gives mixed biblical messages and promotes high-profile celebrity preachers more than it promotes the Lord of Hosts. Still, television can be a powerful medium for the church. Cults have found it to be a successful place; the Mormon church produces highly effective commercials, albeit commercials that distort the LDS's unbiblical tenets by offering the King James Bible to viewers. Still, Christian TV and radio stations have grown from 84 in 1988 to 257 in 1996.[16] It remains to be seen whether these networks and others can provide—or even want to provide—the type of programming that effectively reaches the unchurched.

Another way that TV has been tied to witnessing is through the Evangelism Response Center. Launched by the North American Mission

Board, the center uses volunteers, who answer calls in response to a toll free number. The number is shown in television commercials that are broadcast across the country and that encourage viewers to call.

Two other media also play a roll in reaching the unchurched. Christianity and the radio have, from the early days of radio technology, forged a powerful and effective combination. The other proven media is movie videos. The *Jesus* video, used for two decades by Campus Crusade for Christ, has been translated into four hundred languages and viewed by 1.2 billion people. Over 57 million have reported professions of faith.[17]

The Internet

"The invention of the microprocessor," Sweet declares, "will have a greater impact on planet earth than the invention of fire."[18] Sweet may be exaggerating to make a point, but he's correct in his predictions of a Jetsonlike future: "Before too long, your computer will speak, your TV will listen, and your telephone will show you pictures." And the Internet will influence the lives of my children more than television has influenced mine. In an informal survey, children whose home had computers were asked, "Would you rather keep your TV or your PC?" Seventy-one percent said their PC.[19]

When the Pentagon began "ARAP" in 1969 as a new means to communicate, who could have known its impact decades later? By 1983 a mere 500 computers were connected, but in four years the number jumped to 28,000, and by the year 2000 there were at least 500 *million* hosts: "In 1995 the Internet had 38 million pages; by 2001 the accounts will equal the world population."[20] Most significant in regard to the Internet, however, is not the numbers, nor is it that the Web represents technological advances. Rather, most significant is that the Web has opened horizons for relationships. I carry on a regular e-mail conversation with a man in England about a research project. A few years ago I led my first unbeliever to Christ online, a lady in Oregon who I will likely not meet in person until we are in heaven. This is, indeed, a new world!

Sweet, an astute observer of the Web's applications for the church, notes, "If the technology that led the Protestant Reformation was the printing press, and the product was 'the book;' the technology that is fielding the post-modern Reformation is the microprocessor, and the product is 'the net,' which has been defined as 'an organic combination of hardware, software, and humans endlessly self-balancing.'" Further, "In all of economic history there is no technology that has grown faster than the world-wide web. In 1969 only four primitive Web sites existed in the entire world. In 1990 there were 333,000. By the end of 1997 there were almost 20 million. It took 40 years for radio to reach 50 million domestic users; it took 14 years for television to do that; and for the Internet, 4 years." Then Sweet observes, "It is soon becoming the case that if you had a calling card in the 20th century you will have a Web site in the 21st."[21] That certainly has become the case for me. It is far easier for me to say, "Go to www.alvinreid.com," than to keep up with business cards. This is the language of the emerging youth culture, where teens are more likely to ask your e-mail address than your street address.

Chatrooms are another arena for evangelicalism. Dawn Witherspoon uses her Internet chatroom password as a tool to share the gospel. As minister of missions and evangelism at Simeon Baptist Church, Nashville, Tennessee, she logs onto one of her favorite on-line movie or theater chatrooms with the user name, Connected2Him. "If someone asks me what that means, then, 'Bam,' I have an immediate way to start talking about Jesus Christ,"[22] said Witherspoon.

Witherspoon, who has written a book titled, *Internet Evangelism,* cited immediate ways that Christians can use the Internet as a witnessing tool: People who use e-mail can build an e-mail database that includes addresses of family, friends, church members, and evangelistic prospects. When someone sends them a thoughtful e-mail story relating to Christianity or that would provoke thoughts about faith, they can forward it to people they have entered into their database. She calls this "e-mail for Jesus." Witherspoon said she once sent a friend who was not a Christian one of these types of e-mails. He sent her a return message, telling her the message touched him, and asking her to tell him more. Later, she led him to Christ. "Seventy percent of evangelism done on-line is done through e-mail," she said. Witherspoon believes it is sometimes easier to witness to friends and family via e-mail. "I can write messages that are more clear and thought out than if I were talking to them face-to-face."

When using chatrooms as a venue for evangelism, Witherspoon gives the following hints:

1. Don't be misleading when choosing a name. "Don't represent yourself as a male if you are a female, and don't use a name so obviously Christian that no one will want to talk with you."
2. Maintain your integrity. Be honest.
3. Begin by asking questions.
4. Look for opportunities to share the gospel.
5. Don't be afraid to mention your faith.
6. People who visit chat rooms want to talk.
7. Always ask to exchange e-mail addresses.

Another way people can use the Internet to share Jesus, Witherspoon said, is through evangelistic Web sites. She cited the testimony page (example: *www.heinvites.org*) and the subtle site. The subtle site, she said, is designed as a parable. It does not blatantly talk about Christianity, but it might mention faith issues by highlighting Christian sports figures or addressing nature as God's handiwork. At Southeastern Seminary, beginning the fall of 2002, we require students to spend time witnessing online as part of their studies.

Here are some resources to help with Internet evangelism:

Careaga, Andrew. *E-vangelism: Sharing the Gospel in Cyberspace.* Lafayette: Vital Issues Press, 1999.

———. *eMinistry: Connecting with the Net Generation.* Grand Rapids: Kregel, 2001.

Baker, Jason D. *Christian Cyberspace Companion: A Guide to the Internet and Christian Online Sources.* 2d ed. Grand Rapids: Baker, 1995; *www.web-evangelism.com.*

Missions agencies, too, are recognizing the power of the Web. The North American Mission Board of the Southern Baptist Convention, for example, recently commissioned the first online missionary. One of the evangelistic Web sites the Board has produced for students is www.thekristo.com.[23]

Sports Evangelism

If aliens existed and if a group of them visited the United States to observe the worship practice of Americans, their report might begin with the following:

> The Americans have vast arenas for corporate worship involving thousands of participants in major cities. Those who cannot attend can participate in their homes through viewing screens called television. The worship involves a three-hour ceremony of helmet-clad gladiators who use an oblong object in their ceremony. The priests wear black and white striped garments. The enthusiasm of those in attendance rivals the devotion of few other planets.

Granted, this is a bit farfetched. But the most exciting venue for evangelism today is sports. To start a conversation with an unchurched individual, ask that person about his or her favorite sports team. Through sports personalities, media, events, and competition, the gospel message can ride the world's passion for athletics and for the men and women who compete.[24]

The rationale for sports evangelism is simple: Every ethnic and socioeconomic barrier can be broken with a soccer ball, a basketball, or the athletic tool of choice. Growing up in Alabama, I learned to overlook racial differences on my football team more than at church. The apostle Paul recognized the need to get on common ground with those to whom he sought to share Christ. He wrote in 1 Corinthians 9:22 (NKJV), "I have become all things to all men, that I might by all means save some." And it is interesting that this verse precedes a passage where Paul uses running and boxing illustrations.

Someone has suggested that sports, not unlike Greek in the first century, is the language that all people speak. Sports evangelism allows believers to adapt to the people we're trying to reach, never changing the message, but changing the packaging as needed. Sports can build bridges to the lost. Greg Linville, past president of the Church Sports and Recreation Ministers, identifies six reasons sports evangelism works:

- It attracts the largest cross section of people
- It attracts the secularized, unchurched, nonbeliever
- It reaches two missing people groups: men and teenagers
- It fulfills church growth principles
- People are most easily influenced while having fun
- Athletic facilities attract people

Sports evangelism takes many shapes and forms, most of which can be mixed. But, in general, sports evangelism falls into three categories: event-centered, competition-centered, and personality-centered.

Event-Centered

In the weeks surrounding the 1999 Super Bowl in Miami, the North American Mission Board (NAMB), the Florida Baptist Convention, and Southern Baptists of South Florida partnered to penetrate Broward and Dade counties with the gospel. NAMB was an official cosponsor of the Super Bowl host committee. Hundreds of South Florida Southern Baptists volunteered with the local host committee. Seven churches hosted Super Bowl block parties, and many more had Super Bowl watch parties, with the gospel clearly presented at each. NAMB entered into a partnership with *Sports Spectrum* magazine to distribute 125,000 of their special Super Bowl edition, which were especially crafted for South Florida. Miami Dolphins Hall-of-Fame center Dwight Stephenson shared the plan of salvation on the last page of the magazine, and response cards insured that local churches could follow up respondents. Several thousand responded.

Agencies and denominations all over the world are partnering to reach people for Christ through major sporting events. The Super Bowl, the

Olympics, the Final Four, or your regional high school athletics tournament—all are occasions where lost people gather for fun and fellowship. Christians can find ways to be a part of those events, sharing Christ in a nonthreatening way. Two keys to successful event ministry are volunteers and media resources. One way your church can be of practical help to your community is for members to serve as volunteers with the local organizing committee of a major sports event. Most event managers see the church as a helpful resource. In the course of being a good servant to the host committee, observant volunteers will find many ways to share the gospel. Rule number one is to be a good servant. Then use the opportunity as a bridge to share the gospel.

Competition-Centered

The note had the character only a child could lend. It read,

> Dear Mr. Joe,
>
> Thank you for teaching me about the Lord. I have accepted Jesus as my Savior and was baptized into the body of believers at my church in February. You taught me to love God, and I plan to live the rest of my life for Him.
>
> Your Brother in Christ, Kristopher

Kristopher accepted Christ after hearing his youth-league basketball coach explain the gospel. In competition-centered sports evangelism, the game itself is the bridge. Church recreation softball, basketball, or volleyball opens doors to evangelism, if you avoid the pitfall of having teams comprised of the churched competing against the unchurched. Structure your leagues in such a way that a certain number of unchurched people play on each team, then teach your church members to use the league as a way to share Christ with their neighbors and work colleagues. Better yet, enter your church-league team in the local industrial leagues and take the gospel to the lost.

Competition-centered sports evangelism can also be focused on children and youth. Be aware of the needs in your area for recreation ministry, and then meet those needs with your facilities or with rented or borrowed facilities. During the recent Women's World Cup of soccer, NBC news anchor Tom Brokaw reported that youth soccer leagues all over America had to turn away participants, unable to accommodate the rapidly increasing number of interested youth. Your community may need more leagues, and you can develop a youth sports league that features sharing salvation through Jesus Christ.

That's what Caz McCaslin did in 1994. Since then, his Upward Basketball has erupted into one of the best sports evangelism processes in the world. In the 1998–99 basketball season, 250 churches sponsored leagues in which 48,000 children played. Upward Soccer is being piloted, too, and other sports are being considered. My kids played Upward Basketball, and of the families involved in the inaugural season in 1999–2000, forty-eight were not affiliated with our church.

The gospel is shared at Upward practices, where the coaches lead a devotion at a midpractice break. That devotion is also provided in writing in the Upward Gameplan for Life, a sports New Testament that includes basketball players' testimonies. The gospel is shared at halftime of every game as well. Lay people in the church, parents, coaches, and anyone else who is willing are encouraged and trained to offer a brief testimony about what the Lord is doing in their lives.

Personality-Centered

A lot of people who won't listen to the local preacher or even to Billy Graham will listen to a star athlete. More and more athletes believe that their purpose for being famous is to share the love of Jesus Christ with their fans. David Robinson helped lead the San Antonio Spurs to the NBA title. He enjoys endorsements, fame, and glory. But consider this: "Every time I step on the court, I think about glorifying God," Robinson says. "I just want to make sure people don't think I'm great, but that they think about how great God is. I play so that people can see Christ in me."[25] He'll tell you more if you'll let him. Just go to *www.theadmiral.com*. Or read his testimony in the *Path to Victory New Testament, Sports Spectrum* magazine, or any number of other places, including secular magazines and newspapers that are growing in their willingness to report on the faith of athletes.

Personality-centered sports evangelism works because people love and admire athletes, and many athletes love and follow Jesus. Kurt Warner has had many opportunities to share Christ because of his remarkable MVP season with the Rams in 1999–2000. An internationally recognized leader in the world sports-evangelism movement says that thirty years ago perhaps twenty-five athletes in the world who had at least some level of public recognition were willing to speak out for Jesus Christ. Today there are at least twenty-five thousand. Formula One driver Alex Ribeiro once said, "I had this vision that if I could become world champion, I could reach the whole world [for Christ]."[26]

The concept of personality-centered sports evangelism is incredibly simple, but it has some pitfalls. Start planning for your event long before its date, consider several athletes you might ask to attend, treat them like people instead of superstars (they'll appreciate it), register guests and track who made decisions, be sure that the athlete and the ministry leaders understand how the invitation will be given. For best success, find someone who has had success with such an event and ask for tips. One leader, whose vision has contributed to the success of sports evangelism, says, "There is a remarkable crossing of what has happened on the secular side of sports, the coming to Christ of literally tens of thousands of top-class athletes, and the understanding of the local church that sports is a bridge to their communities. This has resulted in the staggering growth of sports-related ministries by churches and with athletes around the world. God is moving mightily to mobilize the church to cross this bridge."[27]

Sports evangelism has reached around the world. Missionary David Hammond serves as an example of sports evangelism. David's vision involves reaching thousands of youth and adults with the gospel of Christ through sports ministry.[28] Based in the sprawling metropolis of Sao Paulo, one of the largest cities in the world, Hammond and his wife, Aimee, have been serving as international missionaries to Brazil since 1984. The Hammonds targeted *Cidade Tiradentes*, a huge housing complex with two sports centers and one small evangelical congregation. Explaining that *Tiradentes* was built in the early 1980s to relocate people from inner-city slums, Hammond notes, "The people who live there feel like they have been marginalized or neglected by the government."

Decrying the high unemployment, drug use, and rampant crime in the area, Hammond sought to use such tools as basketball and soccer to make an impact. Working in one of the sports centers as well as hosting sports evangelism teams from the States, Hammond says, "Several kids have made professions of faith. One of the boys who accepted Christ is now the assistant to the coach out here."

Southeastern Baptist Theological Seminary, for example, began offering a course on Sports Evangelism in the fall of 2001. Plans are in the works for a concentration, or even an entire degree, in this area.

Evangelistic Entrepreneurs

Mark Cress could be successful in a variety of ventures. But this high-powered businessman left other opportunities to go to seminary—not to become a pastor, however. Instead, he started a corporate chaplains ministry that provides chaplains for secular businesses. The chaplains are trained in counseling, crisis ministry, and other traditional chaplaincy applications. But make no mistake, these chaplains are soul-winners! They are courteous, but clearly evangelistic in their ministries.

The corporate chaplains ministry, called Inner Active Ministries, began in April 1996. In 2000, fourteen full-time and six part-time chaplains ministered to companies with a combined total of over fourteen thousand employees. Also in 2000, these chaplains saw an average of one person come to Christ every day in the workplace. The goal for the next ten years is to place one thousand full-time chaplains in each of the fifty states. The movement has spawned the Corporate Chaplains Institute, which was founded in 1999 with a goal of training over ten thousand workplace chaplains through distance learning. The mission statement of Inner Active Ministries is "to enter the workplace and build relationships with employees with the hope of gaining permission to share the Good News of Jesus Christ with them in a non-threatening manner." You can visit their web site at *www.iachap.org*.

School Evangelism

Columbine exemplifies the need for God in our schools. Yet school is the place in which God is so marginalized that students and teachers must exercise excruciating care to avoid words and images that relate to the gospel. What if, however, public school teachers who know the Lord were equipped, encouraged, and even commissioned to influence their students for the gospel? What if they knew clearly what they could and could not say in the public school setting? (Most do not, so they say nothing.) What if churches began to encourage teachers as well as students in public schools to be missionaries?

The group Audio Adrenaline featured a song calling students to be missionaries. Called "A. K. A. Your Public School," one line says, "They pay to put you in the classes/it's your way to reach the masses."

America's schools are ripe for the harvest. Shouldn't evangelical churches be training the laborers?

Alfred Lloyd Tennyson once asked General William Booth, the Salvation Army founder, "What is the news this morning?" General Booth answered, "The news is that Christ died for our sins and rose for our justification." "Ahh," replied the poet. "That is old news and new news and good news."[29] Seek ways to use the creativity of believers to reach the unchurched with the gospel. Spread the old news—the Good News—in new ways.

chapter ten

Church Planting
Building a Renewed Church
to Reach the Unchurched

IN THE MID 1980S MICHAEL Miller, Phil Neighbors, and Roger Spradlin came together in Bakersfield, California, to start a church. The trio had been friends since their days at Criswell College in Dallas, Texas. Their president at Criswell, Paige Patterson, cast a vision to the students to leave the Bible Belt and plant churches to reach the unchurched. The three took the challenge seriously and headed west. They moved their families to Bakersfield, each serving a separate church. After a struggle, they came together to launch Valley Baptist. Their team approach to church planting, one that closely follows the pattern in Acts, has produced one of the most dynamic, evangelistic churches in America.

Today the church stands as one of the most aggressive, vibrant, evangelistic megachurches in California. Almost three thousand attend worship each week. Mike Miller left the church to minister in the distribution of Christian books and resources; Phil and Roger continue to copastor at Valley Baptist. Valley reaches unchurched people through its doors as well as through several mission churches. How desperately America needs churches like this.

Earlier I stated that no institution in America is more visible yet less influential than the church. In proportion to population there are fewer churches today than there were a century ago. In 1900, there were twenty-seven churches for every 100,000 people in the U.S. In 1950, there were seventeen for every 100,000. At the start of the twenty-first century, there are only eleven for every 100,000.[1]

The most significant strategy to reach the unchurched lies in planting New Testament churches that intentionally seek to reach the unchurched. This strategy is signifcant for two reasons. The first, as just noted, is the decline in the number of churches to the population in America. Second, most established churches will not do what is necessary to penetrate the unchurched culture. Thank God for the many faithful, traditional, loving congregations across the nation that do reach some. But in general, most churches require major retooling in order to focus primarily on reaching the unchurched. I'm an optimist, but I'm also a realist; most will never achieve what it takes.

Hunter observed why traditional churches do not reach the unchurched:

1. Most Christians virtually never reach out;
2. Most traditional churches cannot reach and retain the radically unchurched;
3. Most traditional churches have no plan to reach the radically unchurched;
4. Most traditional churches cannot retain their own children;
5. Most traditional churches fit the culture so badly that evangelism only works sometimes.[2]

To make an impact on the lost culture, nothing less than an assault with the very best of our resources will do. And this is happening. In the early 1990s I served as a denominational leader in evangelism work in Indiana. I learned much about church planting by assisting church planters across the state. At that time, most Southern Baptists thought of church planting as something pastors did when they had failed in established churches. In the minds of many, church planting was a stepchild. Over the past decade an amazing shift has occurred. Now, some of the finest graduates at my school, Southeastern, are intentionally going to places like New England to plant churches, not because they can't cut it in the established churches of the Bible Belt, but because they have a passion to penetrate unchurched areas. The same is happening at many other schools. The evangelical mindset has now turned toward church planting. Now, when attending any meeting concerning evangelism, one hears discussions about church planting as well.

The need for churches that are established specifically to reach the unchurched culture is demonstrated by the following story: A Sheik's four sons returned from studying at a Western University. The Sheik took his sons on a trip through the desert to test what they had learned. They came upon a pile of bones. "Son," the Sheik asked his firstborn, "What did you learn?"

"Those are the bones of a six foot, three-hundred-pound lion," the young man replied.

The father was impressed. He asked his second son, "Son, what did you learn?" That son took the bones and reassembled them into the carcass of a lion. When he asked the third son the same question, he took some hide and put it over the frame of the lion.

When it came time for the fourth son to show what he had learned, he touched the lion and gave it life. So the lion rose up and ate all five of them. The moral: If we don't penetrate the culture, it will devour us.[3]

Church Planting in the Cities

Today, 50 percent of the people in the U.S. live in forty urban centers. Why would God move people to the urban centers of the world? So that we can reach them more easily. In the New Testament, Paul went to the cities to plant churches. In the cities we find the influence of the culture. Jesus saw the city—and He wept for the city. What cities need more than anything is Jesus. As Charles Lyons exhorts, "If you're gonna come to the city, don't bring me psychobabble, bring me a Savior!"

The Armitage Example

The cities of America teem with the unchurched; cities are, indeed, the great harvest field of America. Strategic efforts to plant churches are needed. But another approach is needed as well—the rebirth of struggling, dying churches that have experienced an environment of great change. While not technically a new church plant, such revitalized congregations offer great hope. An example of this is the Armitage Baptist Church in Chicago, which, with its pastor Charles Lyons, was introduced in chapter two.

The greatest opportunity in America lies in her great cities. If you don't think so, don't talk to Pastor Lyons. In fact, Lyons may make you mad. He did not technically start Armitage, but the church was so small and struggling when he came, he approached it as a new church plant.

"When I was called to a little, dying congregation in the inner city of Chicago, it seemed all they were looking for was an ecclesiastical Dr. Kevorkian, but God had other plans," said Lyons. Now a two-thousand-member congregation as diverse ethnically as the city to whom she ministers, Armitage gives a shining example of what the church must do to penetrate the unchurched masses in urban America.[4]

Lyons notes the kind of person God uses in the teeming metropolises of our land. Using Paul's time in the great city of Ephesus as his example, Lyons noted that Paul, like those who are planting churches in the urban setting today, lived by faith in a clear call from God. And Paul simply followed the example of his Lord. "God had determined he would save . . . sinners," Lyons noted. "The plan was that the Word would be made flesh and dwell among us. God did not yell down from heaven, 'I love you.' He wrapped Himself in human flesh and came."

Analogizing Jesus' incarnation to the cities, Lyons observes, "[Jesus] moved into the 'hood,' the worst neighborhood in the universe." The cities are dangerous, some say. Jesus did not come to earth wondering whether it might be dangerous. He came to die. The divine plan of God was to reach the masses of the lost. Where in America are the teeming multitudes? In the cities. "We are losing the battle," said Lyons, "Because we are not following the example."

Could it be that God is organizing America into cities so the church *can* reach more people? Lyons comments:

Which way are you going? . . . While God has been massing His creation in the cities, have you looked around and said, "These folks are not like me. I am out of here"? What must God think of that? White evangelicals from coast to coast have fled the center cities. God put people on our doorstep and we went out the back door. What must God think?

Ephesus serves as a prototype of today's culture. Filled with perversion, materialism, and pagan religion, it sounds like a modern city. But Paul reached the masses through the power of the gospel. Our problem today is that we have become too easily satisfied to live without God's power. What will it take for the established churches in America to cry out in repentance and admit that we have failed to reach the cities? But we must not stop with repentance. We must demonstrate our repentance by penetrating the unchurched areas with new churches.

Juan Rivera—a self-professed "menace to society"—was a crack cocaine and heroin addict who lived across the street from Armitage. In and out of jail, Juan had lost custody of his children. One night the church's sign caught his attention. "Something said in my heart, 'You're going to go there tomorrow.'" The next day Lyons preached on hope. Sick of his four-hundred-dollar-a-day drug habit, Rivera responded to the invitation, saying, "I'd rather die than continue living a slave to what I was doing." Members of the church helped him, some sitting with him Fridays, when in the past he had cashed his paycheck and purchased more drugs. "The people in this church, they showed me something. They showed me that they cared. These people embraced me." Since then, Juan has remarried, bought a house, and regained custody of his four children from their mother, who also is addicted to drugs. "What no program, jail, or anything else did for me, God did for me."

I pray that God will raise up a generation of ministers and laity who will intentionally go to the unchurched in the cities. Would you join me in that prayer?

Penetrating the Urban Culture

Some Southern Baptists are having success in penetrating the African-American culture in the cities. In the Southern Baptist Convention, African-American churches have increased from 1200 in 1989 to 2800 ten years later. In Florida, in the past five years the number of black churches has grown from 100 to almost 300. In Miami, the West Side Baptist Church was a "restart"—a church that had virtually died and was restarted as a black church in 1993. In 1999, twenty-two churches with 2800 members across Miami trace their birth to West Side. Not all of the churches are black. Six languages are represented among the twenty-two.[5] Their experience needs to be multiplied exponentially in every city in America.

West Side Baptist has also effectively penetrated a specific unchurched subculture in Miami—the hip hop culture. Joel Stigale and Dave Web, two youth workers, began the effort. They organized a major evangelistic drive called Generation X Arise. The response was incredible, so the effort continued after the initial drive. Now, a hip-hop group goes to other churches to share how to reach the youth caught up in this subculture.

Attorneys Dan and Helen Sleet exemplify the kind of people God can use to penetrate the unchurched population. Members of the Idlewild Baptist Church in Tampa, Florida, the Sleets, in order to reach more people, left this evangelistic, vibrant, megachurch in order to help plant a church in the downtown area. The new church is as ethnically diverse as the area to which it ministers.[6] More ministers and laity must respond to a similar call from God.

Churches That Reach the Unchurched

My colleague Bill Brown heads our Nehemiah Project church-planting efforts at Southeastern Seminary. We send our students to some of the most unchurched areas in America, such as New England. Bill offers principles for reaching the unchurched through strategic church planting.

A Church Planter/Pastor with an Irresistible Call of God on His Life

Churches cannot grow to greatness while playing ministerial musical chairs. So a pastor must have a sense of God's leading that will endure the discouraging periods every church experiences.

Bill spent almost twenty years serving Alaskan churches. In Alaska, the question asked each new pastor was, "How long are you going to stay?" One man spent seventeen years trying to be called to an Alaskan pastorate. He lasted one wet Alaskan winter. One hundred plus inches of rain was enough for him!

Bill gives an example of an irresistible call:

> Dan came into my office the day after his return from Arizona.
> He and his wife, Jan, had used spring break to visit a prospec-
> tive church plant. I quickly quizzed him about the trip and pos-
> sible plans. Dan spoke about the need and challenge of the area.
> He also stated that without a doubt he did not want to go to
> Arizona. It was hot and dusty. The existing churches were strug-
> gling financially. Dan knew he could do much better after his
> May graduation. Two weeks later Dan again walked into my
> office. His sheepish look pricked my curiosity. Dan looked me
> in the eye and said, "We are going to Arizona." He explained
> that since their return he and Jan had been unable to get the
> people off their minds. Dan knew the irresistible call to shep-
> herd the people that would be reached by his new church.[7]

Do not misunderstand the word *irresistible*. A pastor can resist God's
calling. A pastor can focus on the meager funding, the lack of resources,
or any one of a myriad of challenges facing a church planter. If, however,
the pastor allows his or her focus to be diverted, that pastor will not find
contentment. Joy comes in the knowledge that you are exactly where
God wishes.

Passion for the Lost

In 1998, 154,000 Protestant churches reported no conversions. This
shows a lack of passion for reaching the lost. When one understands the
reality of hell, the holiness of God, the necessity of conversion, and loves
a community, passion for the lost develops.

One of our students at Southeastern explained the source of his
passion in a devotion on the Samaritan woman at the well. He explained how the woman at the well had been publicly embarrassed.
Divorce could only be instigated by the man and was completed by a
public announcement of the woman's failings or inadequacies. After
five attempts, the Samaritan woman may well have settled for living
with a man to preclude further humiliation. Perhaps she had become a

prostitute as a means of support. Then the student added, "There was another woman, Jane, who was married five times. After the fifth marriage she had no way to care for her children, so she turned to prostitution. Finally in despair she put her children into foster care and committed suicide. Jane was my mother. No one ever came to the town prostitute's house to tell her about the living water. No one ever gave her hope and she died. I will never see my mother again, because she died without Christ." Needless to say the Bible study group was stunned. Growing up in a series of foster homes, feeling unloved and worthless, this student encountered Christ. He now has a passion for the lost.

You may be lacking a sense of God's calling upon your life or a passion for the unconverted. You do not have to remain in that condition. Pray that God will supply you with a call and a passion for reaching the unchurched.

Plant a Church That Fits the Community

Kentucky Fried Chicken ads stress that they use the Colonel's original recipe. A decade or so ago a soft drink company spent millions of dollars trying to update their recipe. Problem was, the customers didn't like the change. The company finally retreated to the original recipe. Church planters today must learn the "original recipe" of their area. It's frustrating for a pastor in Alaska when someone from Outside (if you're not from Alaska, you're Outside) says that he or she couldn't find a church like "back home." Every church needs to remember contextualization. For centuries missionaries tried to equate becoming a Christian with becoming westernized. And for centuries Christianity experienced limited success in third world countries. International church planters now promote indigenous churches. It is unfortunate that North American church planters often fail to follow suit.

Franchises may work for chicken but not for churches. Postmoderns tend to reject anything that claims transcendence. In San Francisco, perhaps the consummate post-modern city in the U.S., McDonald's and other national chains fight a constant public relations war. Postmoderns there reject the idea that a chain that fits in Fargo, North Dakota, or

Pearl, Mississippi, will fit in the Bay Area. Know your setting. One pastor rents the local rifle range the weekend before hunting season. His church offers assistance to individuals sighting in rifles, and has contests with prizes. On the range the church encounters men who would never darken the door of a church building. Another friend's church began a 10K fun run in the community. Servant evangelism germane to the locale can earn a hearing for the gospel. Contextualization requires church planters to know their communities and their congregational resources.

The Church Planter Must Build Relationships

When one couple moved onto their ministry field the neighborhood was gang infested. A transvestite lived in the apartment next door. On the other side lived a biker whose girlfriend delighted in trying to shock the pastor's wife. Instead of majoring on the differences, the couple built relationships with their neighbors. Postmoderns see evangelical Christians as narrow-minded, judgmental, and self-righteous. Christians see postmoderns as amoral and intolerant of Christians. These stereotypes can only be overcome by one-on-one relationships. Remember that lost people act lost, so saved people should act saved!

Church planters often go into an area and try to locate as many prospects as possible. Frustration is often the result. International church planters use the term "person of peace" to describe a key indigenous person who is friendly to the missionary's efforts. A large pool of prospects is beneficial, but a person of peace is essential. Pray that God will connect you with a person that can help you learn about the ministry field. That person may not accept Christ during your ministry, but the friendship can help you gain a pastor's heart for your neighbors. Christians must overcome a common temptation—if we can't convert people we reject them. We must always remember that God converts, not us. Learn to love sinners as Jesus did. Love to fish as much as you love to catch. Unless we build relationships with the unchurched, our seeds will fall on hardened ground and result in a small harvest.

What would you or your church do if a transvestite walked into your service? Please understand that in my view a man in high heels is not a pretty picture. But our Savior died for all humankind. The radically unchurched will never walk into our services if we haven't met them outside the building. How can we convey that love to the community? If we cannot honestly say that the church will help individuals and families to build better relationships, will help make the community a better place to live, then we're planting the wrong church.

Remember, postmoderns stress relationships. Many of them grew up in broken or blended homes. They want to succeed in marriage and parenting, but in spite of their intentions, this generation is repeating the relational mistakes of their parents. How can your church help improve families?

God's Word speaks to the real needs of individuals. You can build a new church that reaches the radically unchurched by preaching an expository series from a book in the Bible. But you can add to this. Are there seminars or training you can offer the community to build relationships? In New Hampshire, a mission team saturated an entire town. The single greatest need in the area was identified as a lack of help for youth. Would not a "Parenting Teens" seminar help?

Is your church more than a Sunday morning ministry? How can your ministry express its commitment to the community? Confrontational evangelism must be wedded to relational ministries. A helpful practice is to examine the community activities, determine the underlying value or human need, and then design a ministry that is consistent with the person of Christ and that addresses the value or need. Using a survey similar to that used by Rick Warren when he planted Saddleback Community Church can be a good start.

How Saddleback Began:
A "Personal Opinion Poll"
Taken from Rick Warren,
"The Purpose-Drive Church Conference,"
notes, 15–17 May 1997, Saddleback Community
Church, Lake Forest, California.

Five Questions to Ask
1. Are you currently *active* in a local church?

2. What do you feel is the greatest need in this area?
3. Why do you think most people don't attend church?
4. If you were looking for a church, what kind of things would you look for?
5. What advice would you give me? How can I help you?

Is the community centered around a particular interest, and do you have a related skill that will promote your acceptance in the community? Gary has a ski patrol background that opens doors in Utah. He's able to relate to people on their turf. The first year of Gary's church start, he was called to an avalanche scene to counsel the victims' relatives. Postmoderns will accept your relationship before they accept your religion. And that's how you present Christ—as a relationship.

Bill Brown offers sage counsel:

> For generations ministers were able to live in glass houses with the shades down. Living and ministering within the flock isolated ministers from the unconverted. We were the dispensers of truth seen as spiritual elitists. Postmodern ministry is not so tidy. Christians, and ministers in particular, will need to rub shoulders with the unconverted. And that requires consistency to produce credibility. Institutional Christianity is at least suspect, and at worst rejected. Biblical Christianity validated by an incarnational ministry is viable. And that presents exciting possibilities to a Christian who is willing to live and plant a church within a culture.[8]

God Is Calling Church Planters in an Unprecedented Way

I have observed two exciting phenomena over the past decade. First, the number of churches that take laypeople overseas for short-term mission projects has risen exponentially. Only a few years ago such trips were few and far between. Now, most strong, healthy churches take people overseas annually. The second phenomena concerns the definition of a healthy church. Not long ago, many defined a healthy church as one that grew larger, especially by evangelism. And that's still true. Now, however, more see a healthy, growing church as one that grows by evangelism and by extension—that is, a church that reaches people in her field, while planting new churches in other places. That is a healthy church!

George Hunter recognizes the rise of what he terms "apostolic" congregations, so called "because their leaders are convinced that they are called and sent to reach an undiscipled population."[9] Hunter points to Rick Warren and Saddleback as an example of an apostolic congregation. Saddleback reaches out to the well-educated, influential, laid-back but stressed-out population of Orange County, California. Warren finished his M.Div., then searched out the most unchurched, populated area in America, and planted Saddleback there. Many have followed his lead. "So these churches are apostolic," Hunter states, "in the sense, from the New Testament Greek *aposteleo,* that they are sent out by God to reach one or more distinct populations."[10] Hunter continues: "Today's apostolic congregations are remarkably similar, in certain key features, to the earlier churches that reflected the New Testament, and to the Anabaptist, Pietist, and Methodist apostolic movements within Reformation Christianity."[11] Such churches are literally "churches for the unchurched."

The Role of Church Planting in Reaching Unchurched Postmoderns

Most existing churches are not geared to reach large numbers of the unchurched. The majority of churches in America are neglecting the biblical mandate to reach a lost world. New churches can start out with their primary focus on the Great Commission. Praise God that He can raise a dead church. But to be frank, it is easier to have a birth than a resurrection.

Did You Know?
Did you know that church planting has become
a huge priority among evangelicals over the
past several years? Southern Baptists, for
example, planted 1,537 churches in the year
2000 alone! And did you know that about six in
ten of these new churches were African-
American or ethnic communities?

A biblical rationale for church planting can be found in (1) the Lord's reply to the Great Confession of Peter in Matthew 16, (2) the Great Commission passages, and (3) the doctrine that establishes the New Testament church. Taken together, these three elements explain how the church can bring glory to God. Fulfilling the Great Commission without local New Testament churches is like birthing a baby without a family. In order for the Great Commission to be fulfilled, churches must be planted. Such churches must both be biblical in focus and emphasize evangelism.

Such churches may not be able to "do church" as in the recent past. Because of high property costs, church plants—particularly those in the urban setting—will increasingly find multiple services and remote parking as a normal part of church life. Many urban churches may never own their own building. I've preached in growing churches that have as many as four Sunday morning services, as well as in churches who hold a Saturday night service in addition to three morning services. At one church, the entire congregation came to church on shuttle busses from remote parking areas. Only the greeters and other support staff, along with guests, parked at the church. Churches that seek to reach the unchurched encourage creativity and flexibility among their members.

One of the greatest opportunities for the church today is the rapid growth of massive suburban planned communities, often around a golf course or other interest. These communities include from several hundred to several thousand homes, and are often planned and built with no church in mind. Ted Baird and his family decided to plant a church in one such community named Anthem near Phoenix, Arizona. The Anthem community expects 50,000 residents when it is complete. An estimated 80 percent of these residents are totally unchurched. Planners allowed only four sites for churches for the entire population.

Ted and his family arrived on May 17, 2000, with everything they owned in a rental truck and their car in tow. The next morning Ted awoke to find both stolen! Everything they owned was gone. But as in the story of Joseph, God turned evil into good. The theft resulted in Ted's being interviewed on a local television station—free publicity for Ted's new church.

A block party with about 1000 in attendance kicked off the new Fellowship church. On Easter 2001, 493 attended, with about 115 attending each weekend that spring. Direct mail and a Web site have added to the success of this plant.

Across America, planned communities spring from the soil of virtually every urban area. Most of the people moving to these areas are unchurched. Think of approaching these communities with the fervor of a medical team who are treating a virus. Most of the residents are tainted with the virus of sin; we have the vaccine of the gospel. Ask God what your part could be in reaching them.

A recent development in church planting is one church meeting in two locations. New Hope Baptist Church in Fayetteville, Georgia, where John Avant is pastor, took over a struggling church in addition to the mother church. The second church was essentially restarted as the south campus of New Hope. The senior pastor preaches at both. Hickory Grove Baptist in Charlotte, First United Methodist and Second Baptist in Houston, and others do the same. Almost always the new church is more contemporary, while the established church is blended.

From What Kind of a Church Do You Come?

Tony Campolo is a Christian sociologist. The following account from his life contains implications for church planting. One time he was called from his east coast home to go to Honolulu. Tony was in the hotel the first night and, because of jet lag, at three in the morning he was wide-awake. So he got dressed and went downstairs. He wandered around until he found a small diner, where he ordered a cup of coffee and, in a weak moment, a donut. An obese, unkempt, unshaven man named Harry was working behind the counter. He came out, wiped his hands on his dirty apron, reached into the jar and gave Tony a donut. Tony wished that Harry had served the donut in a different way, but he ate it anyway. Suddenly the door burst open and eight or nine boisterous prostitutes poured in.

The women sat down at the counter next to Tony, and he became even more uncomfortable. But he drank his coffee, tried to look inconspicuous, and listened to the conversation. One of the women said, "Tomorrow is my birthday, I'll be thirty-nine." Her friend replied, "So what do you want from me? I suppose you want a party or something, maybe you want me to bake you a cake?" And this woman, whom he learned was named Agnes, said, "Why are you so mean? I don't want anything from you. Why would I want anything from you? I've never had a birthday party, and no one has ever baked me a cake, and why would I want anything from you? Be quiet." Tony got an inspiration.

Soon the ladies left and Tony said to Harry, "Do they come in here every night?

"Yes they do," said Harry. "Same time just like clockwork every night."

So Tony said, "What about if we throw a birthday party?"

Harry smiled a little, called to his wife, who was back in the kitchen cooking, and said, "Hey, this crazy guy out here wants to have a birthday party for Agnes." They thought it was a wonderful idea.

So the plans were made and everything was set for the party. The next night Tony came back to the same place, same time, finding it decorated with crepe paper and with a sign on the wall that said, "Happy Birthday Agnes."

They sat down to wait and soon people began to trickle in. Word had gotten out on the street. Prostitutes from all over Honolulu converged on the diner, and when Agnes and her friends burst through the door, the place was full. Everyone screamed "Happy Birthday, Agnes!" Her knees buckled a bit, and her friends caught her. She was stunned, speechless, and touched. They led her over to the counter and she sat down. Harry brought out the cake and Agnes's mouth fell open and her eyes filled with tears. They put the cake down in front of her, sang happy birthday, and Harry said, "Blow out the candles so we can have some."

Agnes just stared at that cake. Everyone finally convinced her to blow out the candles, but when Harry produced a knife and told her to cut the cake, she said, "Do I have to? Let me wait a minute." Agnes looked at that cake, so lovingly, like it was the most precious thing she had ever seen, a sacrament of love for her, and she said, "Do I have to cut it?" Harry said, "Well, no, I suppose you don't have to cut it." And then she said something even more strange. She said, "I'd like to keep it for awhile—I don't live far from here. Can I take it home? I'll be right back." They looked at her with puzzled expressions and said, "Sure, you can take it." She picked up the cake and carried it as if it were the Holy Grail. There was silence, stunned silence. Then Tony did something on the spur of the moment. He stood up and said, "Can we pray?"

What an improbable picture this is. A Christian sociologist surrounded by every prostitute in Honolulu in a greasy spoon diner, and he says, "Let us pray." And he did. A simple prayer. He prayed for Agnes, that somehow she would meet Jesus, that somehow she would find salvation, and that God would be good to her, especially on her birthday. He said Amen and the party resumed. Harry said to him, "Hey, I didn't know you were a preacher." And Tony answered, "I'm not a preacher, I'm a sociologist." Harry said, "Well what kind of a church do you come from anyway?" Tony said, " I guess I come from a church that throws birthday parties for prostitutes at three o'clock in the morning."

Harry said, "No you don't, there's no such church like that, cause if there was," he said, "I'd join it."[12]

May God help us to plant churches like that.

conclusion

What Is Your Passion?

THIS BOOK HAS SHOWN BOTH the need and the opportunity to reach the radically unchurched. Along the way you've met a variety of people, many who came from the unchurched population. I'd like you to meet one more such person, Richard Headrick.

Richard is one of my heroes.

It is not that he climbed an active volcano in Guatemala and survived three plane crashes that so impresses me, nor that he narrowly missed being blown up on a train in Peru. Richard is not my hero because he has been shot at, cut with a knife, and faced broken bones and terrorist bombings. I do like a man with an interesting story to tell, but his story is not what makes him my hero. I like Richard's style as a successful businessman who feels comfortable wearing a ponytail and driving a Harley. I praise God for the decision that Richard and his wife, Gina, made to build their new home in Wyoming in the poorer part of their town, rather than among the wealthy. But none of these reasons make Richard Headrick my hero.

Richard is a hero and model for my life because he lives a consuming passion for Jesus. After being radically saved from a pagan background and a sordid past, Richard has become a zealous ambassador for the

Lord. As a member of the Board of Visitors at Southeastern Seminary, he certainly stands out in his ponytail, bearded face, and peculiar means of transportation. But what sets him apart most is his love for Jesus. Whereas he once traveled across the globe searching for earthly treasures, he and Gina now go from country to country to encourage missionaries and to further the gospel.

In my travels and discussions with leaders of the American church, I have come to this conclusion: The single greatest need in the church today is passion. We need, as Jim Cymbala put it, a fresh wind, a fresh fire. Not a wildfire, but fire that brings both heat and light, both enthusiasm and substance. A passion focused on our great God. We need a generation of believers like

- *Isaiah,* who said, "Here am I, send me";
- *Jeremiah,* who despite his difficulties spoke for God, for his Word was like "fire in his bones";
- *Jabez,* whose words spring from the genealogies in 1 Chronicles, crying out for God's blessing;
- *Habakkuk,* who begged God for revival in his day;
- *John the Baptist,* who didn't care if he was antiestablishment, and preached with fire;
- *Wesley,* who said, "Let God set you on fire, and people will watch you burn."

Most of all, we need a passion like that of our Lord, who stretched out His arms and died because of His passionate love for us.

What lights your fire? What feeds your passion? Imagine a generation of believers who seeks to serve Jesus above all else. John Wesley envisioned such believers when he said, "Give me one hundred men who fear nothing but God and hate nothing but sin, and I care not whether they be clergy or lay, I will with them alone storm the gates of hell and set up the kingdom of God on this earth."

Every person ever born has a need to make an impact, has a passion for significance and a desire to do something beyond himself or herself. The desire to honor God is within us all.

Recently my wife, Michelle, and I attended the New Hope Baptist

Church in Fayetteville, Georgia. This great church exudes a passion for God. Such alive, vibrant, and exciting worship! The Sunday we visited, pastor John Avant preached a doctrinal sermon—an effective preacher can make doctrine come alive—on the atonement of our Lord. The time of corporate worship through singing and the message were steeped in passion. It's not surprising that God changed the lives of many people that day. This same church, in fact, reaches many unchurched people in their area. During one summer alone New Hope sent over two hundred of her members on short-term mission trips to foreign lands. Why is this church so effective in reaching the unchurched? In part because a passion for God is seen everywhere you turn.

Do you want to know God's vision for your life? It begins with a passion. It grows with obedience. And it finds fulfillment in honoring Christ.

The word *passion* has gotten a bad rap. What do you envision when you see the word? In our popular culture, one might picture a sultry teen drama on the FOX network, or steamy love scenes from a recent movie, or perhaps even a commercial. But the word *passion* does not necessarily refer to sensuality. One can be passionate about many things. For some guys, it's their cars. For some women, it's their hairstyles.

What is your passion? What drives you? What do people who know you see as the driving passion of your life? When you're alone with only your thoughts, what tantalizes you? What piques your interest? Is there a significant difference between what people see as your passion, and what you are passionate about in your thoughts?

Many people struggle in their walk with God because of passion. *Everyone* is passionate. Not everyone screams their passion; some display their passion calmly, but it is there. And most believers outwardly demonstrate some level of passion toward the Lord. In your heart of hearts, the inner self that only Jesus and you see, what is your passion?

The struggle between our outer and inner lives lies at the center of the spiritual battle we fight on the road to honoring Christ. Have you ever heard about a godly minister who faithfully led his congregation for years and who suddenly abandoned it all in an illicit affair? In many cases, such tragic stories reveal the dichotomy that exists between a person's outer persona and that person's true, inner passion.

When reaching the lost, a passion for Jesus is a prerequisite, because penetrating the unchurched culture will come at a great cost. Many in the church just don't care about the lost, and professing Christians may, in fact, be your greatest opponents when you talk about the urgent need to save souls. Pastors and other leaders who determine to give their lives to reaching the unchurched tell stories of great hardship. But they also tell about the way God moves in power. Penetrating the unchurched culture is not for the faint of heart, but it can be accomplished by the power of God. Let's make an impact for Jesus. Many will thank us in heaven for such a passion as this.

Endnotes

Preface

1. Art Toalston, "Paige Patterson to Chicago Leaders: Baptists to Stay Focused on the City," *Baptist Press Release,* 30 November 1999.

Part 1: A Profile of the Radically Unchurched

1. Leonard Sweet, *Soul Tsunami* (Grand Rapids: Zondervan, 1999), 429.
2. Ibid., 125–26.

Chapter 1: A Brave New World(liness): Who Are the Radically Unchurched?

1. This story is adapted from an e-mail sent by an unchurched friend that the author met on the Internet. Portions of this chapter are excerpted from Alvin L. Reid, "A Hotel for Saints or a Hospital for Sinners: Reaching the Radically Unchurched in America," *Faith and Mission,* summer 1999.
2. Charles Arn, "The State of the Church in the 21st Century," an address presented at the Annual Meeting of the American Society for Church Growth, Orlando, Florida, 13 November 1997.
3. The North American Mission Board estimates agree with Arn: 70 percent of U.S. citizens, or 200 million, are lost. In contrast, the Gallup poll numbers say 81 percent are Christian. Gallup, however, polls those who have a

preference for Christianity, not those who say they have had a new birth through Christ. Barna research estimates that those who have accepted Christ as Savior make up 41 percent of the population. I tend to lean toward the findings of the North American Mission Board and Arn rather than those of Barna or Gallup. See "Are We a Christian Nation?" *Church Planting and Evangelism Today,* spring–summer 2001, 3.

4. George Hunter, *Church for the Unchurched* (Nashville: Abingdon, 1996), 20.

5. See Alvin L. Reid, *Introduction to Evangelism* (Nashville: Broadman and Holman, 1998), 226–28.

6. Research Report Bulletin, Home Mission Board, 1993. The North American Mission Board was formerly known as the Home Mission Board.

7. Hunter, *Church for the Unchurched,* 20.

8. Ibid.

9. Arn, "State of the Church in the 21st Century."

10. Taken from Thom S. Rainer, "Shattering Myths About the Formerly Unchurched," *The Southern Baptist Journal of Theology,* spring 2001, 46–58. The article summarizes findings from Rainer's book *Surprising Insights from the Formerly Unchurched* (Grand Rapids: Zondervan, 2001). Rainer is a dean of the Billy Graham School of Missions, Evangelism, and Growth at The Southern Baptist Theological Seminary.

11. "Snapshots of Islam in America," *Church Planting and Evangelism Today,* spring–summer 2001, 5).

12. Rainer, "Shattering Myths About the Formerly Unchurched," 48.

13. Michael Slaughter, *Out on the Edge: A Wake Up Call for Church Leaders on the Edge of a Media Reformation* (Nashville: Abingdon, 1998), 16.

14. Ravi Zacharias, "Reaching the Happy Pagan," *Leadership,* spring 1995, 18–19.

15. Ibid., 20–21.

16. Ibid., 19–20.

17. Lee Strobel, *Inside the Mind of Unchurched Harry and Mary* (Grand Rapids: Zondervan, 1993).

18. George Whitefield, *The Journals of George Whitefield* (reprint, Edinburgh: Banner of Truth, 1960), 216.

19. Walter Kallestad, *Entertainment Evangelism: Taking the Church Public* (Nashville: Abingdon, 1996), 53.

Chapter 2: A Vision for Reaching the World: What We Are Trying to Do

1. While I heard Sjogran share this understanding at a conference, you can see it detailed in Steve Sjogren, *Conspiracy of Kindness* (Ann Arbor: Servant, 1993).

2. George Hunter, *Church for the Unchurched* (Nashville: Abingdon, 1996), 98.

3. Cited in Arthur Goodrich et al., eds., *The Story of the Welsh Revival* (New York: Revell, 1905), 46. J. Edwin Orr examined the papers as seen in *The Flaming Tongue* (Chicago: Moody, 1973), 15.

4. Leonard Sweet, *Soul Tsunami* (Grand Rapids: Zondervan, 1999), 174.

5. Orr, *The Flaming Tongue*, 5. For a detailed account of Roberts's thoughts see H. Elvit Lewis, "With Christ Among the Miners," in *Glory Filled the Land: A Trilogy on the Welsh Revival (1904–05)*, ed. Richard Owen Roberts (Wheaton: International Awakening Press, 1989), 37–42.

6. This story is taken from the *Net Mentor Manual* produced by the North American Mission Board. It was originally adapted from the "Spider Principle" used in the *Here's Hope Adult Roman Road* manual produced by the North American Mission Board.

7. E. M. Bounds, *Power Through Prayer* (Grand Rapids: Baker, 1972), 6.

8. Alister E. McGrath, *Spirituality in an Age of Change* (Grand Rapids: Zondervan, 1994), 14.

9. Jim Cymbala, *Fresh Wind, Fresh Fire* (Grand Rapids: Zondervan, 1997), 10 (italics added).

10. McGrath, *Spirituality in an Age of Change,* 26.

Chapter 3: The Power of One: The Reason You Live

1. Lynn Vincent, "Gunpoint Evangelist," *World,* 9 October 1999, 16–19. See also Dan R. Crawford, *Night of Tragedy, Dawning of Light* (Wheaton: Harold Shaw, 2000).

2. John Mark Ministries resources for pastors/leaders, at www.pastornet.net.au/jmm/.

3. Ken Walker, "'I Am Not Going to Hide the Light,' Slain Columbine Student Vowed," *Baptist Press Release,* 10 May 1999.

4. Leonard Sweet, *Soul Tsunami* (Grand Rapids: Zondervan, 1999), 114.

5. Ibid., 128.

6. Ibid.

7. From the brochure, "Sing a Little Louder," by Penny Lea.

8. Faith Popcorn, *The Popcorn Report* (New York: Doubleday, 1991), 81.

9. Thom S. Rainer, "Shattering Myths About the Formerly Unchurched," *The Southern Baptist Journal of Theology,* spring 2001, 49.

10. Ibid., 53.

11. Quotation taken from Christian Smith and Michael Emerson, *American Evangelicalism: Embattled and Thriving* (Chicago: University of Chicago Press, 1998). Cited in Peter Steinfels, "Evangelicals on the Rise," *On Mission,* May–June 1999, 12.

12. The following is taken from Alvin L. Reid, "Saying Grace and Being Gracious," *SBC Life,* November 1999.

Chapter 4: We're Not in Kansas Anymore: Why the Church Must Change

1. Lyrics to "Wormboy," by Marilyn Manson, accessed on 5 August 2000 at www.purelyrics.com/index.php?lyrics=zimpiqsw.

2. Taken from a review at one of Manson's official Web sites accessed 5 August 2000 at http://www.marilynmanson.net/news/indes.html.

3. Leonard Sweet, *Soul Tsunami* (Grand Rapids: Zondervan, 1999), 102.

4. I am indebted to D. A. Carson's lecture at Southeastern Baptist Theological Seminary, 8 February 2000, for insights into these eras. For further information see Carson's outstanding book *The Gagging of God* (Grand Rapids: Zondervan, 1996).

5. George Hunter, *Church for the Unchurched* (Nashville: Abingdon, 1996), 21.

6. Ibid.

7. Ibid., 22.

8. Sweet, *Soul Tsunami,* 17–18.

9. Ibid.

10. Tom Wolf, "Postmodernity and the Urban Church Agenda," address to the American Society of Church Growth, 21 November 1997, Orlando, Florida.

11. Jimmy Long, *Generating Hope: A Strategy for Reaching the Post-Modern Generation* (Downers Grove, Ill.: InterVarsity, 1997), 19.

12. Michael Slaughter, *Out on the Edge: A Wake Up Call for Church Leaders on the Edge of a Media Reformation* (Nashville: Abingdon, 1998), 38–39.

13. Sweet, *Soul Tsunami,* 23.

14. Ibid., 288.
15. Ibid., 290.
16. Slaughter, *Out on the Edge,* 38–39.
17. Ibid., 43.
18. Sweet, *Soul Tsunami,* 317.
19. Ibid., 376.
20. Gene Edward Veith, *Postmodern Times: A Christian Guide to Contemporary Thought and Culture* (Wheaton: Crossway, 1994), 144.
21. Ibid., 146.
22. George Hunter, "'Doing Church' to Reach Secular, Urban, Prechristian People," address to the American Society of Church Growth, 21 November 1997, Orlando, Florida.
23. Cassidy S. Dale, "Our Common Future: Scenarios for the North-Central Region of North Carolina 2015 A.D.," Department of Research, Baptist State Convention of North Carolina, November 1998, 23.
24. Ibid., 24.
25. Long, *Generating Hope,* 15–16; 42.
26. Timothy George, "Understanding Postmodernism," presented to the North American Mission Board Conference, Denver, Colorado, 1 December 2000.
27. Long, *Generating Hope,* 211.

Chapter 5: Hope Floats: The Coming Youth Generation

1. Misty Bernall, *She Said Yes: The Unlikely Martyrdom of Cassie Bernall* (Farmington, Pa.: Plough Publishing House, 1999), ix.
2. Ibid., 43.
3. David Van Biema, "A Surge of Teen Spirit: A Christian Girl, Martyred at Columbine High, Sparks a Revival Among Many Evangelical Teens," *Time,* 31 May 1999, 58.
4. John Cloud, "Just a Routine School Shooting," *Time,* 31 May 1999, 58.
5. Taken from Gary McIntosh, *Three Generations* (Grand Rapids: Revell, 1995), passim. The Bridgers information comes from Thom S. Rainer, *The Bridger Generation* (Nashville: Broadman and Holman, 1997), passim.
6. These distinctives come from Neil Howe and William Strauss, *Millennials Rising: The Next Great Generation* (New York: Vintage Books, 2000), 7–10; and author's observations and conversations with student leaders in churches.

7. Jonathan Edwards, "A Faithful Narrative of the Surprising Work of God, in the Conversion of Many Hundred Souls, in Northampton, and the Neighbouring Towns and Villages of New Hampshire, in New England: In a Letter to the Rev. Dr. Colman, of Boston," In *The Works of Jonathan Edwards*, ed. Sereno E. Dwight (London: Banner of Truth Trust, 1834), 1:347.

8. Jonathan Edwards, "Some Thoughts Concerning the Present Revival of Religion in New England, and the Way in Which It Ought to Be Acknowledged and Promoted, Humbly Offered to the Public, in a Treatise on That Subject," in *The Works of Jonathan Edwards*, ed. Sereno E. Dwight (London: Banner of Truth Trust, 1834), 1:423.

9. Lance Morrow, "The Boys and the Bees: The Shootings Are One More Argument for Abolishing Adolescence," *Time*, 31 May 1999, 110.

10. This section is taken from Alvin L. Reid, "Playing Games or Pursuing God," *Southern Baptist Convention (SBC) Life*, August 2000, 7.

11. See Alvin L. Reid and David Wheeler, *Servanthood Evangelism Manual* (Atlanta: North American Mission Board, 2000).

Chapter 6: Add Without Subtracting: Essentials for Reaching the Radically Unchurched

1. Phil Roberts, "Killing Christianity: The Word Under Fire," *On Mission*, May–June 1999, 47.

2. Paige Patterson, Presidential Address delivered to the Southern Baptist Convention, Atlanta, 15 June 1999.

3. E-mail from Thom Rainer to Alvin Reid, 5 June 2000.

4. Thom S. Rainer, "Shattering Myths About the Formerly Unchurched," *The Southern Baptist Journal of Theology*, spring 2001, 53.

5. George Hunter, "'Doing Church' to Reach Secular, Urban, Prechristian People," address to the American Society of Church Growth, 21 November 1997, Orlando, Florida.

6. D. A. Carson, "Athens Revisited," in *Telling the Truth*, ed. D. A. Carson (Grand Rapids: Zondervan, 2000), 392–94. This was also a lecture Carson presented at Trinity Evangelical Divinity School and later at Southeastern Seminary.

7. Ibid., 392.

8. Ibid., 394.

9. Ibid.

10. Colin S. Smith, "Keeping Christ Central in Preaching," in *Telling the Truth,* ed. D. A. Carson (Grand Rapids: Zondervan, 2000), 112.

11. Phillip D. Jensen and Tony Payne, "Two Ways to Live—and Biblical Theology," in *Telling the Truth,* ed. D. A. Carson (Grand Rapids: Zondervan, 2000), 104–6.

12. See Andreas Kostenberger, "Editor's Page," *Journal of the Evangelical Theological Society* 43, no. 1 (March 2000): 2.

13. George Hunter, "The Rationale for a Culturally Relevant Worship Service," *Journal for the American Society of Church Growth* 7 (1996): 137–38.

14. Jim Cymbala, *Fresh Wind, Fresh Fire* (Grand Rapids: Zondervan, 1997), 127.

15. Lynn Waalkes, "Delivering the Message Through Media," *On Mission,* January–February 1999, 44.

16. Jimmy Long, "Generating Hope," in *Telling the Truth,* ed. D. A. Carson (Grand Rapids: Zondervan, 2000), 328.

17. Michael Green, *Evangelism in the Early Church* (Grand Rapids: Eerdmans, 1970), 234.

18. Jimmy Long, *Generating Hope: A Strategy for Reaching the Post-Modern Generation* (Downers Grove, Ill.: InterVarsity, 1997), 194.

19. Thom S. Rainer, *The Bridger Generation* (Nashville: Broadman and Holman, 1997), 166.

Chapter 7: Telling Your Story: The Power of a Changed Life

1. Robert is a student I personally interviewed. His story is used with his permission.

2. Leonard Sweet, *Soul Tsunami* (Grand Rapids: Zondervan, 1999), 202.

3. Thom S. Rainer, "Shattering Myths About the Formerly Unchurched," *The Southern Baptist Journal of Theology,* spring 2001, 52.

4. Faith Popcorn, *The Popcorn Report* (New York: Doubleday, 1991), 245.

5. Sweet, *Soul Tsunami,* 187.

6. D. A. Carson, *The Gagging of God* (Grand Rapids: Zondervan, 1996), 36–37.

7. Dieter Zander, "The Gospel for Generation X," *Leadership,* spring 1995, 40.

8. Cited in Sweet, *Soul Tsunami,* 190.

9. Jimmy Long, *Generating Hope: A Strategy for Reaching the Post-Modern Generation* (Downers Grove, Ill.: InterVarsity, 1997), 188.

10. The material used comes directly from the promotional brochure for the *Net* materials. The *Net* approach was developed by the North American Mission Board of the Southern Baptist Convention and released in 2000.

11. Sweet, *Soul Tsunami*, 215.

12. Rainer, "Shattering Myths About the Formerly Unchurched," 54.

13. Mac Brunson, Chapel Message, Southeastern Baptist Theological Seminary, 25 August 1999.

Chapter 8: Evangelistic Worship: Encountering the Manifest Presence of God

1. Thom S. Rainer, "Shattering Myths About the Formerly Unchurched," *The Southern Baptist Journal of Theology,* spring 2001, 51.

2. "Changed Lives at Armitage," *SBC Life,* June–July 1999, 5.

3. Leonard Sweet, *Soul Tsunami* (Grand Rapids: Zondervan, 1999), 208–9.

4. *On Mission* (May–June 1999), 20 (no author).

5. Sally Morgenthaler, *Worship Evangelism* (Grand Rapids: Zondervan, 1995), 97–122.

6. George Hunter, *Church for the Unchurched* (Nashville: Abingdon, 1996), 67.

7. Melissa King, "Graham Taps Contemporary Christian Music as His 'Interpreter' to Reach Today's Youth," *Baptist Press Release,* 9 June 1999.

Chapter 9: What's New: Communicating Truth in Creative Ways

1. Walter Kallestad, *Entertainment Evangelism: Taking the Church Public* (Nashville: Abingdon, 1996), 10.

2. Ibid., 23.

3. Leonard Sweet, *Soul Tsunami* (Grand Rapids: Zondervan, 1999), 264–65.

4. Faith Popcorn, *The Popcorn Report* (New York: Doubleday, 1991), 168.

5. Steve Sjogren, *Conspiracy of Kindness* (Ann Arbor: Servant, 1993), 209.

6. This approach is popularized in Sjogren's book *Conspiracy of Kindness* and is also called "Servanthood" evangelism.

7. Jimmy Long, "Generating Hope," in *Telling the Truth,* ed. D. A. Carson (Grand Rapids: Zondervan, 2000), 6.

8. Popcorn, *The Popcorn Report,* 121.

9. Sweet, *Soul Tsunami,* 134.

10. Ibid., 136.

11. Byron Spradlin, "Why Are Arts Ministry Specialists So Needed in the Cause of World Evangelization?" *ACTS Perspectives Enewsletter,* May–June 2000.

12. Sweet, *Soul Tsunami,* 25.

13. Tom Wolf, "Postmodernity and the Urban Church Agenda," address to the American Society of Church Growth, 21 November 1997, Orlando, Florida.

14. Sweet, *Soul Tsunami,* 424.

15. Michael Slaughter, *Out on the Edge: A Wake Up Call for Church Leaders on the Edge of a Media Reformation* (Nashville: Abingdon, 1998), 23.

16. Lynne Waalkes, "Delivering the Message Through Media," *On Mission,* January–February 1999, 44.

17. Ibid., 45.

18. Sweet, *Soul Tsunami,* 63.

19. Ibid., 85.

20. Ibid., 86.

21. Ibid., 33.

22. Terri Lackey, "Internet's Rapid Growth Prompts Her Witness as 'Connected2Him,'" *Baptist Press Release,* 30 June 1999.

23. Go to find out more about the NAMB's approach to Internet evangelism.

24. Note: Most of the information from this section comes from Victor Lee's lecture in my class in 1999. Victor is one of the leading authorities in the world on sports evangelism.

25. Victor Lee, "Evangelism Is Not a Spectator Sport," *On Mission Magazine* (September-October 1999): 26–27.

26. Ibid.

27. Ibid.

28. Trennis Henderson, "Missionary Uses Basketball, Tennis to Reach Brazilian Youth and Adults," *Baptist Press Release,* 13 May 1999.

29. Sweet, *Soul Tsunami,* 88. We can share the old news in a new way to reach the unreached.

Chapter 10: Church Planting: Building a Renewed Church to Reach the Unchurched

1. "Are There Enough Churches?" *On Mission,* May–June 1999, 11 (no author).

2. George Hunter, "'Doing Church' to Reach Secular, Urban, Prechristian

People," address to the American Society of Church Growth, 21 November 1997, Orlando, Florida.

3. Leonard Sweet, *Soul Tsunami* (Grand Rapids: Zondervan, 1999), 260–61.

4. Larry B. Elrod, "Following God's Lead, Reach the Big Cities," *SBC Life*, June–July 1999, 5.

5. James Dotson, "Celebrating Ten Years of Starting African-American SBC Churches," *SBC Life*, June–July 1999, 6–7.

6. "On Mission Christians: Their Truth Is More Than Justice," *On Mission*, May–June 1999, 37–38 (no author).

7. Bill Brown, interview by author, August 2001.

8. Ibid.

9. George Hunter, *Church for the Unchurched* (Nashville: Abingdon, 1996), 151.

10. Ibid.

11. Ibid., 152.

12. This story is taken from the audiocassette by Tony Campolo titled, "The Kingdom of God Is a Party" (Nashville, Tenn.: Word Inc., 1991).

Subject Index

Scripture Index

Also by Alvin L. Reid

This compelling book provides an impassioned plea for the church to set their standards higher and reinvent the fundamental ways we minister to teens and their families.

0-8254-3632-X | **208 pages** | **Paperback**

Also by Alvin L. Reid

Many of history's greatest movements of spiritual renewal have been based in radical Christian obedience. Written for young adults, Join the Movement challenges readers to recapture the wonder and majesty of Christian faith and let God fulfill his purposes through them.

0-8254-3652-4 | 160 pages | Paperback | Available March 2007